EMPIRE IN THE EAST

EMPIRE IN THE EAST

EDITED BY
JOSEPH BARNES

CONTRIBUTORS

Owen Lattimore   John E. Orchard

Joseph Barnes   Grover Clark

Frederick V. Field   H. Foster Bain

Carl L. Alsberg   Pearl S. Buck

Tyler Dennett   Nathaniel Peffer

Doubleday, Doran & Company, Inc.
Garden City *1934* New York

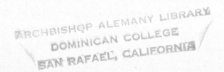

PRINTED AT THE *Country Life Press*, GARDEN CITY, N. Y., U. S. A.

PREFACE

For almost a generation, Americans have been unconscious of the imperial destiny of their nation. When its land frontier had been pushed into the Pacific Ocean, and when an advanced industrial society had taken firm root in this country, it was inevitable that much of the energy and ambition of the American people should turn across the Pacific for an outlet. But it was, in large part, an unconscious process. The fabulous wealth of empire and the God-sent duty to "our little brown brothers" became part of the emotional background of most Americans, but through no act of conscious choice.

Today, we have begun to question the very basis of this empire. The failure of much of its reputed profits to materialize, added to the growing menace of war, has resulted in a spirit of doubt and a disposition to revalue its advantages. The agents of empire, our missionaries, our navy, our diplomats, and our business men, have shaped policies for the United States which are still aimed at imperial expansion. But the appeal to manifest destiny, when its costs are seen to be so high, has lost some of its flavor.

This volume represents a coöperative attempt to state the problems of American policy in the Far East and to suggest some of the possible answers. It has been written at this time because the aims and methods of our advance into the East demand as never before a reappraisal. It has been written in this way because the questions it raises, like the empire it describes, fall into widely differing fields of human activity.

To examine problems as diverse as these is to require the help of many experts. At the same time, it has been imperative that their different points of view be brought into a common focus. Through the American Council of the Institute of Pacific Relations, of which the contributors are all members, it has been possible to achieve this synthesis. When the publishers first put forward a proposal for a coöperatively written book on this subject, it was apparent that the usual form of symposium would not answer. This book has grown not out of a simple assembly of separate essays, but by a careful process of collective criticism and suggestion. This has resulted in an integration which would otherwise have been impossible.

The questions raised in this book have this in common: they lie at the basis of any understanding of our Pacific empire. For several generations, trade, investments, and dependencies have steadily pushed the frontiers of our "national interest" farther and deeper into the East. The export of surplus goods and capital, the search for vital raw materials, and the confident propagation of our ideas and our way of life among Eastern peoples have given us a stake in Pacific affairs and an American "white man's burden."

Although this book is keyed to current problems, it deals with relationships which are more than likely to dominate the struggle for power in the Pacific for many years to come. At the same time, the questions it raises involve more than the foreign relations of the United States in the Pacific. For a modern industrial state, is empire an integral expression of its national life? Is the imperial tendency rooted too deep in the economy and the institutions of the United States to be considered apart from them? For many, this study may raise the question of whether or not our society can much longer endure the strain and pressure which are entailed by its need for empire.

The American Council itself is an unofficial body engaged in long-term research and educational work. It passes no resolutions and works for no specific policies, but for deeper and wider understanding. It has no single or easy answer to the problems stated in this book. It is interested primarily in the development of intelligent public opinion on the new and urgent problems of the Pacific and on proposals for their solution.

Joseph Barnes.

New York City.

CONTENTS

CHINA AND THE BARBARIANS

CHINA AND THE BARBARIANS
Owen Lattimore

THE Japanese intervention in Manchuria in 1931, leading to the establishment of Manchoukuo as a new Asiatic nation under Japanese tutelage, has been all too commonly regarded as a belated example of the type of acquisitive colonial imperialism which characterized the history of Western Europe and America during the nineteenth century, and resulted in the formation of their Eastern empires. It has been deplored as an infringement of the international treaties based on doctrinaire ideas of everlasting peace. It has been regretted as a return to a cycle of history which the Western world thought it had outlived. There has, however, been also a tendency to justify the Japanese on the ground that Japan had entered the comity of Western nations too late to fulfill its history by going through the period of territorial expansion which they had already completed, and the fruits of which they all refuse to surrender, although they feel that they can

[3]

comfortably repudiate the morals of the earlier generations which gave them their heritage. There has been, in consequence, a tendency to hope that the Japanese irruption into Manchuria was the bursting of a safety valve, which let off enough steam to assure the peace of the rest of the world for some time to come.

Any such hope is a smug delusion. The creation of Manchoukuo is not merely the last example of a type of enterprise often undertaken in the past. It marks an epoch, a turning point in history. By definitely establishing the power of Japan on the mainland of Asia (for Korea must be regarded as an approach to the mainland rather than a significant part of it) the factors of land power and sea power in the destiny of China have been brought into full conflict. Since, moreover, Manchuria defines only a part of the land frontier of China, the process begun in Manchuria must spread along the rest of that land frontier, reaching from Manchuria through Mongolia and Chinese Turkistan into Tibet. This does not necessarily mean the extension of Japanese enterprise to such extreme distances; but it does mean a series of adjustments which will define the rest of the open-land frontier as clearly as the Manchurian frontier has been defined, and this cannot be done without war.

Now the whole history of Western empires in the East, from their beginnings, in the sixteenth and seventeenth centuries—in fact, from 1492, when Columbus undertook to open a sea route to the remotest Orient, in place of the land routes dominated by the Turks—has been based on the predominance of sea power over land power. It was the merchants trading at Canton who turned the flank of the Great Wall of China. Only the Asiatic advance of Russia threatened the supremacy of the sea. Japan, by defeating Russia, checked the Russian advance; but in doing so merely took the place of Russia as a menace to Western supremacy. Japan attempted again by the Twenty-one Demands to create a genuine continental position, but again the West, led this time by America, intervened. Since September 18, 1931, however, Japan has created a strong continental position. The land frontier of China once more claims priority over the seacoast, and the Western world must consider afresh the legacy of the position left to it by the overseas expansion of the 19th century, which is now called imperialism—as if it were the only imperialism.

It is therefore necessary to examine the history of the Western impact on China not only as a phase of Western history, but as a phase in the history of China. It is not too much to say that the history of Western encroachment on China should be considered as an interlude between periods in the history of the Great Wall.

For more than a hundred years the nations that call themselves "the civilized world" have looked forward to the "modernizing" of China. Repeated disappointment has not led, so far, to any general restatement of the problem. It is still assumed that the Chinese are a backward people of arrested cultural development, who need only to be brought forward from a half-medieval condition to the high standing of modern civilization. Yet the truth of the matter is that the Chinese have a culture of their own which in most respects is far

[5]

more advanced and mature than that of the West. Where it suffers by comparison with the West, it is more often because of the decay of a standard that was once higher than because of failure to develop to a standard sufficiently high. The problem which is commonly stated as one of developing China up to the Western standard can be much more clearly stated as one of destroying the standard of China in order to substitute that of the West. The relation of China to the West can no longer be discussed in terms of parallel development. It must, if it is to be understood, be treated as a frontal conflict.

Nor is the culture of the West the first alien culture that has attempted to break in on and dominate China. For centuries the Chinese have been under severe pressure from the north, from the "barbarians" beyond the Great Wall, who have repeatedly conquered or controlled China and have greatly modified the political tradition of the country but have never altered its underlying cultural life. Successive periods of submission to alien political control, during which Chinese culture withdrew as it were into itself, living under the shell of barbarian rule, have, in fact, hardened the unreceptive tradition of the Chinese. Each period of defeat was followed by a time of barbarian recession, in which the Chinese were able to rule themselves, and Chinese culture, emerging again into political freedom, was able to renew something of its old vigour.

This alternating cycle of repression and release, dominated by the wars and migrations of barbarian peoples beyond the Great Wall, established so powerful a rhythm in Chinese history that it affects to this day the relations between China and the Western world. In the nineteenth century, the impact of the Western nations along the coast of China developed with comparative suddenness from private ventures which often had a smell of piracy about them into a general pressure which threatened to control or even to divide and rule the whole of China. It was almost inevitable that the Chinese should transfer to these new "sea barbarians" the whole stock of traditional forms of resistance and avoidance which had been developed through many centuries of history, in which both the domestic affairs and the foreign policy of China had been overshadowed by the "land barbarians" of the Great Wall frontier. The type of opposition to barbarism had become so engrained in Chinese life that it is now impossible to appreciate the innermost discords of the relation between China and the West unless allowance is made for what one may call the Great Wall tradition, and unless it is recognized that, for China of the Chinese, the problem of the West is a modern equivalent for the earlier problem of the barbarous tribes ranging between Tibet and Manchuria.

China, on ordinary maps, is marked and coloured as a country about the size of the United States, with the addition of Alaska and Mexico; but the population is not evenly distributed over this enormous territory. There are no accurate records of population in China; the Chinese, exclusive of Mongols, Tibetans, and so forth, may number anywhere between 400 and 500 million. About 28 million of this total are Chinese living in Manchuria; the rest, numbering roughly four times the population of the United States, are confined within an area less than half that of the United States. This is the true China, sometimes referred to as China proper, or China within the Great Wall. It is less than half— less than three eighths, in fact—of what is marked as Chinese territory on the maps.

The rest of what is nominally Chinese territory comprises the Outer Dominions, which approximate to the United States in size. Of these Manchuria is one sixth, Mongolia one half, Chinese Turkistan one fifth, and Tibet one sixth the size of the United States. It is about as far from Dairen across Manchuria, Mongolia, and Chinese Turkistan to Kashgar as it is from New York to San Francisco, and they are roughly in the same latitude. The non-Chinese population of these territories includes Manchus, Mongols, Central Asian Turks, and Tibetans, who are not only un-Chinese in race, culture, and language, but for the most part are anti-Chinese in tradition and national feeling. The Manchus, owing to Chinese assimilation, are a partial exception. These peoples number anywhere from 7 to 17 million. The statistics are even less reliable than they are for China proper, but one thing at least is clear: the total number of non-Chinese peoples in Greater China does not even equal the number of Chinese living in Manchuria.

This brings us directly to a problem which, if rightly understood, is one of the master keys to Chinese history: the balance of power between Chinese and barbarians. It is the natural and easy assumption of most Westerners, in considering the *modern* problems of China, that given the heavy concentration of Chinese in the comparatively small area of China proper, and the ridiculously thin and scattered population of Greater China, there must be an enormous pressure outward from China proper into the frontier lands.

It is therefore all the more important to make it perfectly clear that almost throughout history there has been no such pressure. The empty frontier, on the contrary, has always had a pronounced tendency to bear down heavily on the crowded heart of China. The building of the Great Wall marks an epoch in Chinese history, and the Great Wall, as a unified frontier, is more than two thousand years old, while the earliest fortifications which preceded it were very much older.

It was under the Ch'in dynasty (249–206 B.C.) that the frontier was consolidated. Thereafter, under the Han dynasty (206 B.C.–A.D. 221), the Chinese settled down to a permanent type of culture, a permanent ideal of domestic life within China proper, and a permanent attitude toward the frontier and the barbarians. Since then they have been a people homogeneous in race, language, culture, and political tendency. From that time onward genuine and permanent expansion toward the north has never been a characteristic of Chinese history. The major trend of Chinese expansionism has always been toward the south. It is in the south that the Chinese have "digested" each successive conquest, making land and people and culture permanently, characteristically, and unmistakably Chinese.

In the north, on the other hand, the power and influence of China beyond the Great Wall have always been precarious. Even in periods of maximum expansion—as when, for instance, the Han dynasty carried the influence of China far into central Asia—the system of control was based primarily on alliances with non-Chinese peoples, whom the Chinese were unable to conquer outright, much less to displace by colonization. The real trend of what may be called Great Wall history has always been in exactly the opposite direction. The Wall itself, conceived as a system of defense and carried out on a scale to fit eternity, indicates that when the Chinese were working out the form of their empire and the scope of their culture they felt these trans-frontier regions to be beyond them. The barbarians had for centuries been thrusting forward against China, and in fact it may well be said that the Great Wall, generally considered the greatest monument of the power of China, was primarily an acknowledgment of the power of the barbarians.

Nor did the building of it put an end to barbarian pressure. The Chinese, under the Han dynasty, by making use of barbarian counter alliances, turned the Hsiung-nu or Huns away from the Great Wall; but other barbarians, tribe after tribe, maintained the tradition of barbarian supremacy over China. In the seventeen hundred years between the end of the Han dynasty and the present time, there have been a round thousand years in which parts of China within the Great Wall, and sometimes the whole of it, have been ruled by conquering alien dynasties from beyond the Great Wall. Even when China was ruled by the Chinese, the barbarians were often powerful enough to dominate frontier policy, although their power was disguised under the fiction that they were "allies" or "tributaries."

The cycle of barbarian invasion and Chinese recovery had become so permanent, so normal an element in Chinese life by the time that the appearance of the Western nations interrupted it, that the Chinese inevitably and spontaneously transferred to their relations with the "barbarians of the sea" the complete stock of ideas, feelings, policies, and methods which had been developed by centuries of opposition to the Great Wall barbarians. The maladjustment between China and Western civilization during the nineteenth and twentieth centuries turns largely on the fact that both Chinese and foreigners were attempting to apply preconceived "stock" ideas to a situation that was radically new.

For the Westerners also attempted to meet a new situation with ideas that had developed under fundamentally different conditions. Almost all Western studies of China are vitiated by the practice of applying to Chinese history and civilization, Chinese forms of dynastic structure, law, social order, war, nationalism, revolution, and so on, the concepts developed in the West out of Western history.

China, in the nineteenth century, when the West began its long series of fumbling attempts to create a China policy, formed part of the Manchu Empire. The West built up its China policy on the assumption that "China" and the "Manchu Empire" were the same thing. From this misconception there sprang a series of badly geared policies which now threaten to wreck the Republic of China and the peace of the Far East and the world.

The Manchu Empire was, in structure, an incorporation of China in an empire ruled from north of the

Great Wall. China was a "possession" of the Manchus, but Manchuria, Mongolia, Chinese Turkistan, and Tibet were not "possessions" of China. The rise of the Manchu power, leading to the conquest of China in 1644, was grounded on alliance between the Manchus and the Eastern Mongols. They made good their position within the Great Wall by conquest. North of the Great Wall, they had to fight at different times against Mongols, Central Asian Turks, and Tibetans; but these were wars which resulted in a primacy of the Manchus among the tribal peoples, very different from outright conquest. Alliances and the granting of privileged status were as important as war in the formation of this trans-frontier grouping.

The Mongols, the Central Asian Turks (together with other Moslem groups, for Islam ranked within the Manchu Empire as a *nation* rather than a faith) and the Tibetans, all considered themselves in some degree allies of the Manchus and partners in the dominion over China. They were all descendants of races which at one time or another had made conquests of their own within China, and the regions in which they lived had never "belonged" to China permanently or been inhabited by Chinese in any large numbers. They were ruled, or rather administered, from the Manchu court at Peking in a manner which made it perfectly clear that their standing within the Empire was different from and higher than that of the Chinese. They had almost an associative or participative position, and it was the general policy of the Empire to limit contact between them and the Chinese in order to prevent them from being assimilated by the Chinese.

CHINA AND THE BARBARIANS

The impact of the West brought about a substitution of sea power for the tribal land power which had always impended over Chinese history. The Manchu Emperors, having moved their court to Peking, had already a tendency to regard themselves as Emperors primarily of China. As a result of this attitude, they had begun to turn their historic position as overlords of a trans-frontier group of non-Chinese nations into a system of alliances and counterbalances which would prevent any other people, like the Mongols, from supplanting the Manchus as the chief military race beyond the Great Wall, while allowing the Manchus to retain their position as rulers of China.

This tendency was turned into an anti-frontier movement by the Western nations, which by reason of their approach from over the sea were ignorant of the Great Wall rhythm in Chinese history, and could not in any case be interested in the regions beyond the Great Wall until they had dealt with the immediate problem of China. Western activity destroyed the old balance between China proper and the regions that are now called Greater China. Railways and modern armaments were the chief instruments of this reversal. China became, for the first time, superior to the land barbarians in military power. Railways reduced the difference in mobility between nomad horsemen and the slow armies of China, and modern arms gave the Chinese a decisive advantage over such peoples as the Mongols. These peoples had stood still during the rule of the Manchu dynasty, confident in their association with the Manchus and their privileged position within the Empire, and unaware, because of their distance from the sea, that the world was being changed by the invasion of strange powers along the coast of China.

When the Manchu Empire fell and the time came for the next great movement of peoples and readjustment of power, they found the Chinese, who had immemorially been incapable of wide positive expansion beyond the Great Wall, facing them with an overwhelming advantage in arms. China, moreover, stood between them and the sea, over which came the main supply of arms. Russia was the only foreign nation which by virtue of its position could maintain the historic importance of the land frontier—and for this reason, indeed, the relations of Russia with China have always been different from those of any other foreign nation. Russian influence in outer Mongolia and central Asia has made the Russians, from the point of view of Chinese history, the new dominant "tribe" beyond the Great Wall. Russia, however, was somewhat held in check by the other foreign powers, for, in so far as the group of Western nations had a common interest, it was as much opposed to Russian expansion up to the frontiers of China proper as it is now distrustful of the unsettling of the sea-power factor in Chinese affairs by Japanese expansion on the Continent of Asia.

The smothering of the Great Wall frontier by the power which China drew from the West resulted finally in one of the most extraordinary situations in all Chinese history: the proclamation of the Chinese Republic and the recognition of a Chinese title to sovereignty in Manchuria, Mongolia, Chinese Turkistan, and Tibet. The West, far from realizing the extraordinary character of the situation thus created, took it all as a

matter of course—a beautiful example of the application of stock ideas to a radically new problem. International practice, from at least the time of the Treaty
of Nanking in 1842, had come squarely to the point
of treating the Manchu Empire as if it were the Empire
of China. This led as a matter of course to the assumption on the part of the Western nations, when the
Chinese Revolution of 1911 overthrew the Manchu
Empire *in China,* that China stood heir to the Manchus
and could claim the "possession" of the Outer Dominions.

There is no doubt whatever that the Mongols and
the Tibetans, the two most solid national groups affected by this historic reversal (for the Manchus as
a race were already in decline, owing to assimilation
with the Chinese, whom they ruled), regarded the fall
of the Manchu Empire as the destruction of a framework, which ought simply to have allowed the original
component parts of the Empire to resume their own
national identities. Nor can there be any doubt that
legally and historically they were right. They had
never "belonged" to China, and had the cycle of history
gone on "normally," without the intervention of the
West, the fall of the empire would have left a China
independent of barbarian control, and a group of "barbarian" nations standing free either of commitments
to Manchuria, to each other, or to China—at least,
until the next period of frontier wars.

The Chinese Revolution, indeed, began instinctively
with an admission of the quasi-federative character of
the old empire. Its early policy was to *persuade* the
Outer Dominions to maintain a federative relation to

the republic. Its five-barred flag symbolized the union (in equality) of Chinese, Manchus, Mongols, Moslems, and Tibetans. The shift toward assertion of a Chinese monopoly in sovereignty over the Outer Dominions came later. It was encouraged by the foreign policy of treating China as the owning element in the republic, and by the growing realization, within China itself, that under current conditions the overwhelming advantage lay with the Chinese. The final step was taken by the Nationalist government, which entered on a forward policy inspired with the idea of "China *and* the Outer Dominions for the Chinese." It abolished the five-barred flag of federation and equality, urged the assimilation and absorption of non-Chinese peoples, and began to divide up the more accessible regions of Mongolia and Tibet into Chinese provinces, governed without reference to the separatist feelings of the non-Chinese inhabitants.

The foreign attitude toward the republic was not only a convenience. It was regarded as essential to the balance of world peace before 1914. Russia was eager to assert a special sphere of interest in Chinese central Asia, outer Mongolia, and northern Manchuria. Japan claimed a special sphere in southern Manchuria and the part of inner Mongolia that overlaps into Manchuria. British interest preferred a nominal Chinese sovereignty over Tibet and Chinese Turkistan, because the frontiers of the Indian Empire are more secure with a weak nation standing between India and Russia. To have recognized not only special interests of this kind, but a separate national character in each of the regions affected, would have brought the rivalry of the

[16]

powers concerned too dangerously into the open, besides interfering with the special American hobby of the Open Door. It was more discreet to work on an assumption of Chinese sovereignty, and to exercise pressure on Greater China indirectly, through China proper.

Moreover, the Western world at that time could see no future for China except under Western guidance (a term conveniently vague); and by confirming a maximum area for China it increased the sphere of future Western investment and exploitation. Thus there was established, in spite of the violence done to history and to the non-Chinese peoples from Manchuria to Tibet, the fiction of a Chinese Republic that overflowed from China to the borders of Siberia, far into central Asia, and over all Tibet; and thus were laid the foundations of an unreality that will be the cause of Asiatic wars all through the twentieth century.

More than half of the fictitious China thus created was an anomaly, and an anomaly that in the light of history was almost incredible. Only the Mongol dynasty of the Yuan (1260–1368) had ever ruled a "Chinese Empire" greater in extent than the new Chinese Republic. No dynasty of genuine Chinese origin had ever ruled anything like so far beyond the limits of China proper. Yet the West, having recognized the title of China to these unwieldy dominions—having indeed virtually presented them to China—very nearly made possible the implementing of the title. For in so far as Chinese claims beyond the Great Wall have been made good at all, they have been made good by Westernization. They are the work, above all, of railways and firearms, which were themselves to begin with, and to a great extent still are, the marks of Western domination over China.

Except for the small and very old Chinese *enclave* in southern Manchuria, almost the whole of the Chinese expansion and colonization beyond the Great Wall dates from the twenty-two years of the republic. Railways and armaments began to take effect in China with abrupt rapidity after the Boxer Rising of 1900, which was a desperate revulsion of Chinese feeling against the unwanted wonders of the West. They had a great deal to do with bringing on the revolution. Their effect in promoting colonization beyond the frontier, in spite of disorder within China itself, created an easy belief (the West being always optimistic about the benefits of Westernization) in an approaching "rebirth" of China. It was assumed that the Chinese, of their own energy, were on the point of transforming the vast regions that were only nominally Chinese into a Greater China homogeneous with China proper.

In the shadow of this belief the fact that the nations of the West, intruding on China from the sea, had taken over the function of the land barbarians as the anti-Chinese factor in Chinese history, was lost to sight. Yet, in point of fact, Chinese expansion beyond the Great Wall meant simply the extension beyond China proper, by the Chinese themselves, of the very alien forces that were threatening China, and which the Chinese within China were trying to evade, or to nullify by balancing one foreign agency against another. It meant an enlargement of terrain, but not a change in the nature of the conflict. It meant the conquest of the outer, nominal China, by the real China—on behalf of the West. The Western assumption that China was expanding by reason of its own pent-up energy, for which the West had provided only the means, was therefore a shallow fallacy; for in fact the West was providing, throughout, not only the means but a great part of the impulsion. Chinese expansion was, to some extent, a recoil, compensating for the shock of Western pressure on China proper.

The judgment of history is now being shown forth. The expanding land frontier of China, being a creation of the West, or a result of Western action in China, could be held only so long as the West, as a whole, was willing to prevent any one foreign nation from interfering with the Chinese advance. The Chinese were set in motion during the period of great Western activity and confidence which ended in 1914. They continued to gather momentum even after the unity of the West broke down in war. They reached their maximum of expansive effort only after the Washington Conference of 1922, when the West, suffering from the effects of war, was at its minimum of energy. China, comparatively free from fresh Western pressure, then reached its highest point in the use of Westernization by Chinese for Chinese ends. Then, in conflict with Russia in 1929, and again with Japan in 1931, it became evident that Chinese-controlled Westernization had overshot the mark. Chinese expansionism collapsed inward on itself, and relations between China and the barbarians came to the end of one phase and the beginning of another.

Westernization, as the chief hope for the rehabilitation of China, is at a deadlock. The forces of the land frontier, which were superseded so recently by the Western sea powers, have come into play again, and the fate of China turns now on the balance between sea barbarians and land barbarians. The Japanese policy in Manchuria means that Japan has broken away from the group of Western sea-power nations and is attempting to create a continental position. If the attempt succeeds, then the place of Japan as a sea power may become secondary and defensive, while Japanese continental policy forces a reconsideration of the future of Asia. It is this momentous alternative which underlies the strain and uncertainty of political thought in Japan today.

The reëmergence of the land frontier in Chinese affairs makes imperative a fresh approach to the problem of the "foreign barbarians" as a force in Chinese history. It is necessary to study the equivalence, or alternation, between land barbarians and sea barbarians, from the point of view, primarily, not of Western thought, but of Chinese history, the growth of the Chinese culture, and the Chinese way of life. The Western aspect of Westernization, as a method of solving the problems of China from the outside, has been given too much weight, as against the Chinese aspect, in which "reform" and "development" are offset by the implications of surrender, and the destruction or submergence of essential Chinese values under a new form of barbarian conquest. The grossly self-complacent Western confidence in "modern civilization" finds it difficult to see anything but constructive and progressive values in Westernization, where Chinese thought and Chinese feeling see profit and technical progress offered at the price only of unsympathetic destruction and a terrifying confusion of moral values. Foreign ways of thought, especially if they have to be adopted out of necessity, may be a form of foreign control as oppressive as political domination.

For two thousand years, indeed, for some three thousand years, reaching far back into the incompletely documented and semi-legendary epoch of the Chou dynasty (1122–255 B.C.), China has been dominated by the same wilderness frontier that survives in our own day. The northern defenses which in their final form became the Great Wall frontier marked off a limit for the culture and the people of China as well as for its power. Although they prided themselves on their superior civilization, their manufactures and arts, their noble literature and high canons of thought, the Chinese were at a disadvantage in the unending struggle to stave off barbarian invasion.

In the ages of bow-and-arrow warfare the crudest barbarians could match themselves against the most mature civilization. There was no such disparity as there is now between savages and the troops of civilized nations. In Chinese history, indeed, the major advantages lay with the barbarians, whose attacks could damage very quickly the economic organization of a civilized country like China. Military expeditions from China against the barbarians, on the other hand, were enormously expensive and could guarantee no permanent results. The barbarians were nomads who could withdraw before a Chinese army as it advanced and turn to harry it as it retired. Barbarian armies paid themselves in the loot they found in China, while

Chinese armies cost the state far more than it could possibly win by successful marches through the empty pastures of the nomads. This type of opposition between "barbarism" and "civilization" was not, of course, peculiar to Chinese history. It was a factor also in the history of Egypt, the Roman Empire, and Mesopotamia.

Barbarian invasion therefore hung over China as a permanent threat, which was frequently realized in conquest. It became a rule in Chinese history that the freedom of China did not depend on political unity and soundness of administration within China—as is usually assumed—so much as on disunity among the barbarians. Any barbarian nation that could guard its own rear and flanks against other barbarians could set out confidently to invade China.

Since even the best organization and military training could give China only the negative advantage of a successful defensive position along the Great Wall, there grew up inevitably a canon of statecraft and foreign policy based on the assumption that fighting the barbarians was less efficacious than promoting confusion among them—by intrigue, by bribery, by alliance, by hiring some of them as mercenaries against the others, by any possible means—in such a manner that, being involved against each other, none of them would be free to attack China. This is the celebrated canon of *I i chih i*, "using barbarians to control the barbarians," which is fundamental in Chinese history.

What has not been generally enough appreciated by Western students of Chinese history, however, is the reverse application of this rule: that good government at home is less vital to the nation than successful intrigue abroad. The foreign and domestic policies of any nation are external and internal facets of a single phenomenon. If foreign policy is based on the assumption that courage and direct action are useless, then courage and initiative cannot be the guiding characteristics of internal policy.

China has thrown off, with a vitality which is the admiration of all historians, the *individual* effects of one after another of its periods of subjection to foreign invaders. Nevertheless, the *general* effect has left a deep wound in the life of China. Even the soundest culture cannot throw off entirely the general effects of chronic defeat and repeated subjection, and it is now impossible to understand the character—as distinct from the structure—of Chinese civilization without reference to this aspect of its history.

From the unendingly repetitive cycle of barbarian conquest and Chinese recovery there sprang, moreover, a strongly marked convention of strictly limited cultural interchange and racial assimilation. It is an axiom of Chinese history that barbarian invaders have always tended to merge into the Chinese population and become Chinese. The converse of this axiom is equally true, but has never received anything like the same emphasis. It is that Chinese who have penetrated beyond the Great Wall have always tended to become "tribal." Instead of creating a genuine "Greater China" they have always inclined to associate themselves with the power of the frontier and to turn inward on China.

Thus peoples who have crossed the Great Wall have regularly assimilated each with the other; but the

[23]

frontier cleavage between nations and tribes, cultures and races, has never been obliterated. The Mongols who entered China during the Mongol conquest left very little trace; the Mongols who remained in Mongolia are still Mongol, and still stubbornly antagonistic to the idea of becoming Chinese. The equivalent phenomenon within China is the unwillingness of the Chinese to modify their standards permanently in order to deal with any barbarian intrusion. The Chinese nation has always relied on its ability to underlive and outlive conquest. The ability to survive by suspended animation has taken precedence over the ability to master the problem itself.

For twenty centuries at least there has been no creative development within China. There have been only cycles, representing variable applications of a single cast of feeling, permanent in type, to problems that were treated as if they were eternal and inalterable. Whenever the Chinese were conquered, the normal reaction of their culture was to go underground until the conquerors had turned Chinese, when it came to the surface again, as Chinese as ever. Nor, when restored to freedom, did it take steps to solve the barbarian problem permanently and prevent future defeat. It simply repeated the rebirth, growth, and decay of similar periods in the past.

Thus generation by generation the already established and unreceptive character of Chinese culture was confirmed and hardened. This quality of stubbornness, compounded of a superficial willingness to yield and a fundamental unwillingness to change, passed over into the relations between China and the West. The elusive underlying problem of Westernization has been the reserve of vitality in Chinese culture, enabling it to withdraw and retire within itself during the period of Westernization, with the hope of being able to emerge again after the forces of Westernization have been spent.

There has, however, always been a fringe of "regional" peoples along the frontier whose function was to coalesce with the barbarians when the barbarians were on the advance, and with the Chinese when China was on the recovery. The records of the north are filled with the names of barbarians who went over to the Chinese, and of Chinese who went over to the barbarians, and in so doing became potent agents in the success of invasions and the fate of dynasties. Nor is it adequate to put the name of traitor to such men and so dismiss them. They were symbols of the uncertainty of allegiance in their own times, and turned one way or the other, according to the set of the tide of history in their own generation. So, and in the same way, we find Alsatians of German name commanding French armies, and Lorrainers of French name high in the service of Germany. The equivalent of this modification of national character in our own day is to be found in the Chinese who has become a kind of secondary foreigner, and whose effect on his own country approximates to foreign conquest as it were at one remove. Foreigners who have become "secondary Chinese" have had little to do with the fortunes of China, however, for as yet there is no tradition of ebb and flow in the relations between Asia and the West.

The head-on conflict between China and the West

during the nineteenth century originated in Western attempts to make China adopt Western standards, while the Chinese, falling back on the classical policy of "using barbarians to control the barbarians," would go no further than trying to play off one Western nation against another, and one Westernism against another, in order to allow the old standard of China to survive intact. Most of the failures of China in this period were due to the assumption that the traditional methods evolved in face of the land barbarians were the only methods adequate or necessary for use against the sea barbarians, and to the failure to appreciate essential differences between the two kinds of barbarians. It took several defeats in open war, ending with dictated treaties, to remove the term "barbarian" from documents officially communicated to the representatives of foreign nations. Even the tradition that internal weakness or strength is less important to the safety of the state than spreading confusion among the barbarians has not yet been abandoned. This is the only explanation of the fact, otherwise inexplicable in Western terms, that so extreme an emergency as the Japanese invasion of Manchuria produced only half-hearted efforts to achieve unity in China, while all Chinese worked with vigour to set against Japan the power of the League of Nations, of Russia, of the United States—of any nation but China.

In other respects, however, the situation in the twentieth century is much more complicated, because at least the coastal fringe of China has actually been Westernized in part, with the result that the forces of a half-Westernized China can now be used, alternatively, against the old China and against the West itself. Such forces are a contemporary equivalent of the half-Chinese, half-barbarian frontiersmen who from time to time in the history of the Great Wall have thrown their weight on the side of China or the side of the barbarians. They stand in the full tide of history, and according as the West increases its activity in China or relaxes, unwilling or unable to keep up the pressure, they may serve as agencies of further Westernization or of anti-Western reaction.

The railways and armaments introduced into China were marks, in the first instance, of defeat. They have since become pivotal factors of the exercise of power within China by Chinese; but this does not necessarily mean that they have lost their potency either as disruptive agencies of foreign aggression or as agencies to be turned by China against the West. As for the immemorial frontier of the land barbarians, it was first in great part overwhelmed by Westernization, and then transformed into a new frontier, quite as dangerous to China proper as the old.

Railways and armaments made possible a Chinese expansion beyond the Great Wall which almost succeeded in abolishing the old method of alliances and diplomatic control. Until then, there had never been a mass movement of Chinese toward this frontier. Chinese colonization beyond the Great Wall, as a major phenomenon, dates only from the last thirty years. Until the building of the railways, the only Chinese community beyond the Great Wall that was important in numbers and at the same time genuinely old and permanent was in southern Manchuria; and it had been made possible by use of the lower Liao River and the coastal trade routes. During the long centuries of Chinese advance into the Yangtze Valley, and beyond it into the deep south—the historic direction of Chinese conquest and imperial growth—the economic development essential to the complex Chinese civilization of city life associated with intensive agriculture had been made possible by coastal trade and inland waterways. Beyond the Great Wall, only Manchuria had a coast and inland waterways of any importance; but even here the growth of a community genuinely Chinese in type was limited to the southern peninsula and the lower Liao, because the rest of the inland waterways favoured Siberia or Korea rather than China. All along the Great Wall, west of Manchuria, Chinese colonization had never become genuinely expansionist. The agricultural settler, without waterways, was prevented by distance and poor transport from reaching an export market.

The building of railways made expansive colonization possible. Manchuria and southern Mongolia became granaries offering very large profits to those who exploited them. Such people as the Mongols could, for the first time, be not only defeated but driven out or exterminated and replaced with a permanent Chinese population.

The old frontier regionalism, on the other hand, reasserted itself in a most remarkable manner. The regions of Chinese expansion beyond the Great Wall have consistently been hostile to the control of the central government. If they acquire wealth, and especially if they acquire railways, they arm themselves at once and take an independent stand in the intricate shifting of alliances and civil wars which may be called the prime phenomenon of Chinese public life.

In so doing, they necessarily turn inward on China, reasserting over China the old regional domination of the trans-frontier barbarians. The more "modernized" the frontier region, the heavier its impact on China. In Chinese Turkistan, with no railways, a poor supply of arms, and a small Chinese population, the Chinese who rule over Central Asian Turks and Western Mongols have been content with a wary balance between maintaining their status as a ruling race, and evading all liability to control or taxation by the government of China.

In Manchuria, the Chinese have been for some time a compact, homogeneous, and overwhelming majority. They had almost obliterated the Manchus and were encroaching steadily on the Mongols—about a quarter of Manchuria is even now held by the Mongols. They had a far greater mileage of railways in proportion to territory than any part of China proper. They had arsenals, a free supply of munitions from abroad, and one of the most formidable armies in China. All these advantages they used to create a regional power that was virtually autonomous, and whose most conspicuous activity was its repeated invasions of China proper, making parts of northern China tributary to it and over-awing the central government. Before the Japanese invasion, it is true, Manchuria had "submitted" to Nanking, but on terms that more closely resembled an alliance than recognition of superior power and authority.

Within China itself, Westernization is also a double-edged sword, cutting one way against the unity of China and one way against Western domination. The great hinterland of China, and the heart of the country, hate and fear the Treaty Ports, of which Shanghai is the head and forefront. The most efficient enterprises of foreign type directed by the Chinese themselves have still to be carried on under the lee of the Treaty Ports and the foreign concessions. No National government can stand independent of the Treaty Ports—especially because of the customs revenue that is collected there under the supervision of foreigners who rank as Chinese government officials. The mass of the country, however, suspects any government that relies on this "foreign-tainted" money.

No progressive government can stand in China unless it stands for Westernization, and for the control of China by the Westernized minority. No progressive government, therefore, can survive if it is cut off from the Treaty Ports, which are the sources of Westernization; and every progressive government, therefore, is under suspicion in the far interior, which fears that the Westernized Chinese may be the forerunners of Western aggression.

For Westernization has brought about, in China, a series of the most complicated contradictions. On the one hand, it tends to fasten Western control more firmly over China. Even Chinese agencies of Westernization are dependent to a certain extent on foreign assistance, or at least on foreign goodwill. On the other hand, Westernization is a chief cause of disruption. Hardly a civil war is fought without direct reference to railways, by which troops can be moved and along which revenues can be collected, or to arsenals, or to seaports, through which foreign munitions can be obtained.

The whole career of a man like Feng Yü-hsiang, the "Christian General," whose tale of alliances and betrayals is to the ordinary Westerner an inexplicable series of irrational treacheries, becomes quite simple if interpreted against the background of un-Westernized China. He is a kind of folk hero of the recurrent Chinese instinct to use Westernization for the purpose of breaking away from the West. He is a representative leader of the hinterland, distrusting the "modern" leaders of the coastal region and distrusted by them. His career has been a succession of attempts to break through from the hinterland to the coastal railways and coastal ports, in order not to be starved of munitions by his rivals. For the sake of reaching the coast—or an overland supply of munitions from Russia—he has always been ready to make alliances of convenience with any Chinese faction or Western agency, and equally ready to denounce them. For the purposes of such a man, Christianity is little more than a strategic Westernism, an adjunct of military discipline, and a device for making his armies incompatible with other armies, and thus difficult to win away from his control.

In China, again, the Westernizers are in some degree an equivalent of the "tribalized" Chinese who in times past shared in barbarian conquests of China—like the "Chinese Bannermen" who served with the Manchu armies. They are, therefore, in the same way, dependent on foreign alliances, and their Westernization can be, and sometimes is, nothing but a short cut to power in China. Viewed in this light the modernizing Chinese is a kind of "secondary foreigner"—a definition which ironically but not without justification recalls the epithet of "secondary foreign devils," applied to Chinese Christians at the time of the Boxer Rising of 1900. This accounts for much of the violently destructive character of the revolutionary movement in China and the corresponding weakness and indecision of its creative faculty. Not that the Chinese are peculiarly sluggish in the organic amalgamation of Western and Chinese thought. The smattering of Chinese philosophy that was fashionable in eighteenth-century Europe, in the Age of Reason, for instance, was never anything but external decoration, and never affected the internal evolution of European philosophy.

Westernization, however, acts also as the vehicle of the most vehement anti-Western feeling. The most patriotic and most constructive Chinese are those who are committed primarily to the emancipation of China from foreign control, and only incidentally to Westernization, as a means of using the powers of the West against the West. By the standards of such patriots, the only safe policy of Westernization is one of "countersapping" against the West, by the use of what has been learned from the West. By this I do not mean the comparatively limited opportunism of a Feng Yü-hsiang, so much as anti-Western Westernization of the kind recently employed in Manchuria. The use of the Chinese railways in Manchuria to offset the power exercised by Japan through the South Manchuria Railway (and, to a lesser extent, the Russian interest in the Chinese Eastern Railway) proved so nearly successful that it had a great deal to do with bringing on the crisis of 1931.

Refusal to surrender China to the discretion of the West can only be called a noble ideal. To accept Westernization as the West sees it would mean the abandonment of all Chinese pride in things Chinese. Westernization at the discretion of China means holding off the West until China can be admitted to equality of standing, and until the West recognizes that the Chinese have a right to their own cultural standard. The highest ambition possible for the present generation of Chinese is an equality of technical accomplishment as between China and the West, together with total independence of the cultural foundations of Western technical achievement—a difficult ambition. China may be modernized but must not be barbarized.

This means that so long as the Chinese feel there is a hope for China they must work for jealousy and disunity among the Western nations. No harmony between the Western and the Chinese points of view can be expected. The Chinese practice of twenty centuries and more in making such concessions to the barbarians as might be unavoidable, but without putting China on the same plane as the barbarians, continues to operate. What the West thinks of as modern civilization (the *only* civilization), the Chinese are inclined to think of as a collection of useful technical processes oddly associated with an inferior civilization.

It is not surprising that China should have been more interested in the products of the West than in the type of civilization that created them. It was easy to assume that the Chinese could learn to profit by

Chinese or foreign, who had the power to take and to hold. It would certainly bring on foreign intervention, either in the form of political adventure, or for the sake of peace—a kind of late-Roman imperialism, undertaken more out of necessity than from ambition.

Because Western civilization has never seemed to China as a whole what the West thinks it ought to be —an obvious progression from backwardness to efficiency—there is no general agreement within China itself either on the necessary degree of Westernization or on the method of achieving it. There has been, in consequence, an erratic opportunism in all attempts to deal with the West—tentative, doubtful, overemphatic one year, and hastily abandoned the next. The fashion swings from social reform to economic revolution, from military organization to international negotiation, from boycott to financial coöperation. The modernists tend to become more and more destructive, pulling down the old China before the means of building a new nation and culture are available. The conservatives tend more and more to accept only cash value in the innovations that they employ, distrusting all new ideals and keeping the old alive by shifts and expedients. The pressure of world history, in the meantime, throws into increasing opposition the forces of the old trans-frontier barbarian lands, now coming under the influence of newer barbarians like the Russians and the Japanese, the forces of the sea barbarians of the West, and the forces of the true ancient China, which was once a civilized world of its own, self-created and self-sufficient, the "Central Nation" of the world.

THE JAPANESE DILEMMA

THE JAPANESE DILEMMA
John E. Orchard

JAPAN today stands isolated, condemned by world opinion, withdrawn from the League of Nations, feared as a menace to the peace of the world. Military operations are being conducted on the mainland of Asia, and relations with Russia are strained. A trade war with Great Britain is in progress. At home there is much talk of conflict with the United States. Restlessness and confusion are evident in the activities of the patriotic societies, in criticisms and attacks directed against the political parties and the great commercial families, and in proposals for a reorganization of the government and for a greater control of industry by the state. All this turmoil arises from the failure of the process of Westernization to bring economic security.

Poor in resources essential to the new industrialization, Japan is dependent upon imports, if there is to be any expansion of manufacturing, but imports cannot continue without exports, and Japan seeks to expand markets in an age of contracting world trade. The dilemma in its realities has been present in the background for several decades, but it has been fully appreciated only within the last few years. The answer has not been found. In seeking it, Japan may turn to further military conquest, to some form of state capitalism, to a lowering of the Japanese standard of living to meet the competition of the other countries of Asia, or to a more aggressive search for markets aimed at displacing the West completely in the Orient. Any one of these alternatives would have a significant bearing upon America's trade interests and upon American policy in the Far East. But whatever the course chosen, it will be directed, and its effectiveness will be limited, by the fundamental economic position of Japan.

It is not seeking too far for origins to find the seeds of Japan's present difficulties in the forcing of that country's closed door by the Western powers in 1853. For two and a half centuries, Japan had lived in seclusion. Foreigners had been expelled, Japanese were not permitted to leave the country, and contact with the rest of the world was limited to a very closely supervised trade with a few Dutch and Chinese merchants. Within the narrow confines of a small group of islands there had developed a practically self-sufficient state with institutions fixed in the rigid mold of tradition and changing slowly, if at all. In contrast, it was for the European nations a period of rapid political and industrial development accompanied by a most active expansion with colonization and wars for trade and territory.

Japan remained passively aloof from all this competition. It is true that at an earlier time the world of

Japan had been wider. Japanese armies had invaded Korea, and Japanese pirates and merchants had penetrated to Southern seas and had acquired considerable influence in the affairs of Java, Siam, Cambodia, and the Philippine Islands. In these excursions abroad the Japanese had come into contact with the spreading power of the Portuguese, Spanish, Dutch, and British; and if foreign intercourse had been permitted to continue, it is possible that the course of events in Asia might have been altered drastically. But with the seclusion edict of the Shogun early in the seventeenth century, the Japanese adventurers either returned to Japan, or their settlements gradually faded away and were lost in the native populations. In time Western expansion reached the shores of Japan, and finally isolation was ended by an American fleet in search of trade privileges. The intrusion was not welcomed. Even in the face of a superior force, a considerable body of opinion demanded that resistance should be offered to the barbarian invaders. Other leaders were no more ready to receive them, but they did appreciate the futility of attempting to meet modern weapons with the arms at their disposal, and they were sufficiently familiar with the improvements that were being made in means of communication to recognize that even if the American force could be turned away it was only a question of time before pressure from Russia or France or Great Britain would put an end to isolation and bring Japan into intercourse with the world.

Once Western expansion had broken down the barriers, it was inevitable that Japan should become an active participant in the struggle for territory and markets. Passive resistance to Westernization might have been possible for a larger and richer area, but for Japan there seemed to be no other course than to adopt what the West had to offer and use it, if possible, as a defense against further encroachments. Change became the order of the day. Ancient political and social institutions were destroyed or altered. The government was reorganized. There was a new interest in other countries and other peoples, and possible dangers in neighboring lands were visualized. The modernizing of the Japanese army and navy was begun. Industries of the factory type were established. Many of these developments demanded material resources that Japan did not possess. They were sought abroad, and in return Japanese goods found their way to foreign countries. Japan was soon embarked upon the same process of expansion and the same search for markets that had brought the Western nations to Asia.

In the changes that have occurred in Japan in the last seventy-five years or so, perhaps the most notable has been the development of manufacturing industry of the Western factory type. There had been a beginning of industrialization in the years immediately preceding the opening of the country, but it had been limited to the establishment of arsenals and shipyards by some of the feudal lords, either in the hope of preserving isolation or in anticipation of its termination. Factory industry may be said to date from the introduction of 6,000 cotton spindles from England in 1859 and their installation in a mill near Kagoshima in southern Kyushu. Other factory industries followed, including the reeling of silk, iron- and steel-making, paper-making, brewing, the rubber industry, the match industry, and the making of chemicals. As was to be expected, manufacturing developed slowly in the earlier years, but at a gradually accelerating pace and with particular stimulus during such periods as the Russo-Japanese War and the World War.

There was little for the new industry to build upon in Japan. During the previous centuries the dominant occupation of the country had been agriculture with from eighty to eighty-five per cent of the population dependent upon the land either as farmer peasants or as landowners and feudal lords. Though the great majority of the people led an extremely frugal and simple life, a limited demand for fabricated goods did exist. To meet that demand, there was some industry, but it was of the handicraft type. It included the spinning of yarn, the reeling of silk, the weaving of cloth, the preparation of foodstuffs such as sake, shoyu, fish delicacies, rice, and tea, cabinet-making, pottery-making, the forging of swords and armor, the working in such metals as bronze and copper, certain other industries to supply the everyday needs of the people, and a few art industries catering to the wealthy and to the nobles of the court. These industries were all carried on in households or in workshops employing four or five workers. With the exception of the luxury goods, the products were consumed in the neighborhood where they were manufactured, for there had been little development of communications beyond porter and pack horse, and it was not possible economically to transport bulky articles any distance. The workers were artisans and craftsmen. Though they might be highly skilled, they had little knowledge of the use of metal in construction or in machinery. They were not mechanics, and for the new industry mechanics were demanded. In short, Japanese manufacturing was in a stage of development somewhat similar to that prevailing in England in the seventeenth century. It was called upon to effect almost immediately a change that had been spread over two or three centuries in the West and to make the jump from the workshop to the factory and machine, from the artisan to the mechanic and the engineer, and from wood as the principal material of construction to iron and steel.

Retarding this abrupt transition and hampering the development of the earlier industries there were three major obstacles: Japan did not possess the knowledge of machine technique or of large-scale factory management; there was no body of labor with the required skill, and the supply of capital for the purchase of the necessary new equipment was scanty. There were, however, certain advantages that tended to offset these obstacles in some degree. Japan could draw upon the accumulated experience of the West, and many of the pioneering steps in industrialization could be eliminated. The private capital of the country, though limited, was concentrated in the hands of a few powerful families closely related to the government, and it could be directed easily into industry. And finally, the feudal period had given to Japan a strongly centralized government and to the people a great respect for authority and a dependence upon it. It was natural to expect the government to take the initiative in the modernizing process and to follow its lead. The government provided the capital for the new means of transportation and communication and for the establishment of many of the new manufacturing industries either through grants and subsidies to private interests or by direct government participation. Other industries were started by the powerful Mitsui, Kawasaki, Sumitomo, and two or three other wealthy families, and they later acquired many of the government plants.

The government dispatched Japanese abroad to study Western industries, and many foreign experts were brought to Japan from America and Europe to teach the new technique in manufacturing. From France came Paul Breuner with reeling basins for the raw silk industry. British engineers built the first railroads. British workmen assisted in the erection and operation of the early ironworks and cotton mills, and British teachers conducted a school in glass-making in Tokyo. British and American engineers introduced modern mining methods and the use of explosives. Swiss were brought in to establish the hemp-braid industry. German experts introduced the brewing industry and later the smelting of zinc and the making of steel and chemicals. French and German specialists were used in the dyeing plants. There are few industries in Japan today that did not draw upon foreign experience in their earlier years, and few industries that are not directly indebted to government encouragement. So active has the government been in industrialization that even at the present time industry turns first to the government for assistance in case of difficulty.

During the earlier years of the modern period, industrialization was directed primarily toward the building of a nation sufficiently powerful politically and economically to take its position among the nations of the world on terms of equality. Gradually a second incentive began to assert itself. With the throwing off of the constrictions that had hampered the country during the feudal period, one of the most striking results has been the rapid increase of the population. Since 1873 it has doubled, and in 1932 the increase was a little over one million. In view of the limited area of the country, Japan is faced with a serious population problem. In a territory smaller than the state of California, there is a population of almost sixty-seven million or a density of 450 per square mile. Five sixths of the country, however, because of its rugged, mountainous topography, is not arable, and the population density in relation to the area that can be utilized for agriculture is some twenty-seven hundred per square mile. No other important country is quite so crowded.

To meet the problem thus presented, a number of solutions have been suggested or attempted. Emigration to the less densely populated portions of the Empire and to foreign countries has been encouraged, but the results have not been impressive, partly because there are so few lands open to Japanese settlement, and partly because the Japanese have never shown themselves to be pioneers willing and able to meet and overcome frontier conditions. There are at present fewer than 600,000 Japanese—or less than the net increase of a single year—living outside the Empire who can be considered as emigrants; and in the last decade or so, the number seeking repatriation has exceeded the number leaving the country in most years. Despite the present elaborate plans for colonization in Manchuria, there is a growing conviction in Japan that emigration offers no solution to the population problem.

Important improvements in agriculture have been accomplished. The yields of rice and other staples have been greatly increased, and considerable areas of land have been reclaimed and made arable. There are limits to such improvements. Little idle land remains that can be brought into cultivation at a cost within reason. In recent years the government has announced ambitious plans for reclamation, but in the most optimistic schemes the annual increase in arable land is placed at only 75,000 acres, while 142,000 acres would be required to grow the rice alone for the population increase of each year. As a matter of fact, the land under cultivation at the end of 1931 was 275,000 acres less than in 1925.

The per acre yields in Japan, due to intensive cultivation and the liberal use of fertilizers, are in general greater than the yields in other countries, and it is not probable that the soil can be made to produce in much greater quantity. In other countries agricultural production has been increased through the introduction of machinery, but the tiny fields of Japan and the limited areas of level land are a bar to the use of any large machines. It is conceivable that the continued extension of machinery into new lands may even add to the difficulties of the Japanese farmers, for such extension will tend to hold agricultural prices to a low level, and the Japanese, with their more costly hand methods, will find it increasingly difficult to compete. During recent years there has been a great deal of suffering and discontent in the rural areas of Japan, and unless some highly successful plan of relief can be devised it is likely that the movement of the population will be away from the land rather than toward it. Certainly, at the present time, it does not seem probable that the solution of the population problem will be found in agriculture.

Other countries, notably Great Britain and Germany, have provided support for a crowding population through the intensification of the use of their land by the developing of manufacturing industries. It has become increasingly evident that industrialization offers the most promising solution of this important problem in Japan, and in recent years more and more emphasis has been placed upon the development of manufacturing industries.

The trend of industrialization has been strongly influenced by the available raw materials. Japan is a poor country. Not only is the area of agricultural land limited, but the islands possess few of the essential raw materials for manufacturing that have contributed to the growth of such nations as Great Britain, Germany, and the United States. With the shift to the machine, power becomes all-important, and despite the development of water power and the use of petroleum, power still means coal. Japan has some coal. The reserves remaining in the earth are estimated at about 7.5 billion tons. At first glance, this total would seem to be an ample supply, but for so large a population it is quite inadequate. In per capita reserves, Japan ranks far below the industrial countries of the West. Even at the present very low rate of consumption,

Japan's reserves will be exhausted in less than two hundred years, and at the per capita rate that coal is being consumed in Germany, they would be exhausted in about forty years. Not only is the supply deficient, but the coal is expensive to mine, since it lies deep and in thin seams, and very little of it will make a satisfactory coke for the blast furnace. If industrialization is to progress in Japan to anything like the degree it has in Western countries, either coal must be imported or a new source of power must be discovered.

Some petroleum is produced along the west coast of Honshu, the main island of Japan. The annual output is small, and in 1932 equaled for the entire twelve months only about 70 percent of the yield of the petroleum fields of the United States for a single day. The domestic production does not meet the demand, and in recent years more than 80 percent of the *petroleum* consumption has been imported. There is little expectation that additional fields will be discovered in the Japanese islands, since the geological formations are known to be in general unfavorable to the occurrence of petroleum. In view of the greatly increased use of petroleum in merchant and naval vessels and in airplanes and motor vehicles, the dependence upon foreign sources has become a matter of grave concern. Much attention is being given to acquiring control over adequate supplies both through exploration work in Japanese territory and through the penetration of Japanese capital into foreign fields. There is every indication, however, that dependence must continue to be upon imports.

The same rugged topography that has limited agri-

worked under conditions of the present day. The total
reserves of the country are small and have been estimated at about 80 million tons with perhaps one half
of the ore unsuitable for modern furnaces. Even under
the pressure of the World War, the maximum annual
production was less than 400,000 tons, and usually it
is around 200,000 tons. In the United States, the annual
consumption of iron ore for the years preceding the
abnormally low year of 1932 ranged from 30 to 75
million tons. The reserves of Japan are quite inadequate
for the development of an iron and steel industry. If
it were necessary to supply the iron and steel requirements of the country entirely from domestic deposits,
all of the Japanese iron ore, both high and low grade,
would be consumed in less than twenty-five years. The
progress of the industry in the past has been based
mainly upon imported ores. Any future expansion must
depend upon imports to an even greater degree.

The other minerals mined in Japan in important
quantities are copper and sulphur. Copper was practically the only commodity exported during the centuries of seclusion. As late as 1923 Japan ranked third
among the copper producers of the world, surpassed
by the United States and Chile. The Japanese mines,
however, have been worked for a very long time, and
it has been difficult for them to compete with the low-
cost deposits opened recently in Africa, Canada, and
South America. Japan now ranks fifth as a copper producer, and it has become increasingly difficult for
Japanese copper to compete in world markets with the
low prices that have prevailed since the World War.
Exports have fallen off, and since 1919 they have been

exceeded by imports. It is probable, however, that the copper reserves are ample to meet the requirements of the country for many years to come, providing the consumers are willing to pay the higher prices.

Sulphur, an important raw material in the fertilizer industry, occurs in many places in connection with the chain of volcanic formations extending throughout the length of the Japanese islands from northern Hokkaido to southern Formosa. Despite the abundance, costs of mining are much higher than in the very easily worked Texas and Louisiana deposits, and it would be more economical for Japanese industries to set aside the Japanese deposits for use in case of emergency and to depend for normal consumption upon supplies imported from the United States.

The climate of Japan is well suited to the cultivation of the cotton plant, and at the time of the opening of the country it was a crop of such importance that many of the early foreign visitors predicted that Japan would shortly become one of the leading sources of raw cotton for the textile mills of the world. But little cotton is grown at present. The demand upon the arable area for food crops has been too great, and practically all of the raw cotton now consumed in the Japanese cotton industry is obtained from the United States, India, China, and Egypt. With the adoption of Western styles of dress, there has been a growing demand for wool cloth, and a wool-weaving industry has been established to supply a part of that demand. Though efforts have been made to encourage the raising of sheep, they have not been very successful, chiefly because of unsuitable pasture. There are in Japan

Plans were formulated in 1905 for the settlement of one million Japanese colonists in Manchuria in the next ten years, but in 1930, twenty-five years later, despite the growing pressure of population in Japan proper, there were in all of the region only 250,000 Japanese in a total population of over thirty million. They were concentrated mainly in the cities and were engaged in trade or connected with the South Manchuria Railway or the government. The more rigorous climate of the mainland, the unfamiliar agricultural conditions, and the competition of the Chinese farmers with their lower standard of living had discouraged emigration.

Economic development of the controlled area was pushed by Japan, particularly the exploitation of mineral resources. The output of coal from the open-cut mines at Fushun was increased greatly. With low production costs, it was possible to send the coal southward along the coast of China and up the Yangtze Kiang as far as Hankow. A part of the output was shipped to Japan, though the coal is not of coking quality and could not meet one of the difficulties of the Japanese iron and steel industry. An iron plant was established at Anshan by the South Manchuria Railway and another at Penhsihu by a private Sino-Japanese company. The Penhsihu plant has been fairly successful, though the output is small. The larger plant at Anshan has experienced serious difficulties from the beginning of operation. The reserves of ore are large, but the quality is so low that in most Western countries there would be no attempt to use it. Costs of production at the plant have been very high, and the pig iron has been of such unsatisfactory quality that it has been

difficult to find a market for it. Japan has continued
to import pig iron from India despite the much longer
haul.

At the coal mine at Fushun, a few years ago, a plant
for the distillation of oil from shale was established. It
is operated on a highly favorable contract with the
Japanese navy to take the entire output at cost, but
the commercial success of the plant is questionable. If
operated at full capacity, it will supply Japan with less
than 10 percent of the annual consumption of petroleum.

The South Manchuria Railway, largely due to revenue derived from the transport of Fushun coal and
north Manchurian wheat and beans, has been a highly
profitable enterprise, but its hold upon Manchuria was
challenged by a system of competing Chinese lines that
was nearing completion in 1931 and was able to carry
Manchurian produce to the sea quite independently of
the South Manchuria line. Traffic was being diverted to
the new lines, partly because their rates were quoted in
silver while the South Manchuria rates were in gold,
and partly because of the preference of the Chinese ship-
pers. The South Manchuria Railway was responsible for
the establishment of a number of manufacturing industries in the railway zone, but most of them were unable
to compete with Chinese industries and were forced to
close down.

The Chinese have never accepted Japanese control
in Manchuria. Resentment has grown, and every opportunity has been taken to obstruct and hamper. If
it had been possible to strike a balance in the summer
of 1931, it would probably have been revealed that
Japan had attained her political aims in preventing

the control of Manchuria by a strong power, but that economically the whole adventure faced complete failure. Huge capital investments had been made upon which there was little prospect of return. Chinese enterprises were steadily gaining ground. Chinese farmers occupied the land. Chinese traders were monopolizing the buying and selling of Manchurian staples, and Chinese commodities were displacing Japanese in the Manchurian markets. In Japan there was the realization that despite the degree of the Japanese hold, sovereignty over Manchuria remained with China, and control, in so far as there was any documentary basis, was only temporary. Japanese private capital was slow to move to Manchuria, particularly prior to the extension of the term of the territorial and railway leases to the end of the century by the Twenty-one Demands of 1915. In trade, Manchuria was foreign territory, and goods shipped to Japan were subject to import duties exactly as were those received from the United States, India, or any other country. Dependence upon raw materials from such a source was considered too precarious a foundation upon which to build great manufacturing industries.

The military activities begun in September, 1931, were the answer of the Japanese army to the situation in Manchuria and to the threat of economic failure. Chinese sovereignty has given way to a nominally independent state with Japan in control. Through the breaking of the Russian hold in northern Manchuria, important strategic advances over Russia have been gained, but this advance has made more imminent a second Russo-Japanese war. The possibility of competi-

tion from the Chinese-owned railways has been removed
by their consolidation into one system with the South
Manchuria Railway. Access to the coal and iron ore
and the beans and wheat òf Manchuria in the event of
war has been assured.

But these gains are mainly political, and the economic
gains are less apparent. Japan has been for a number of
years the principal market for Manchurian agricultural
produce and has experienced no difficulty in obtaining
all her requirements of the particular foods raised in
Manchuria. It is not probable that the new policy
toward Manchuria will increase materially this trade
in agricultural products.

The new policy will not give coking properties to
Fushun coal, nor will it improve the quality of Anshan
iron ore or lower the production costs of pig iron. It
will not ensure the successful commercial operation of
the oil distillation plant. It is not probable that it will
give to Japan any important quantity of cheap cotton,
despite the efforts that are now being made to extend
the cultivation of the cotton plant in Manchuria. It
may increase the supply of raw wool and meat. Plans
for Japanese colonization have been revived, but few
in Japan, outside the military, place much hope in
them. There has been no change in the climate; agricultural methods are still unlike those practised in
Japan, and the competition of the Chinese is keener
than ever, since migration from China in recent years
has been at the rate of five or six hundred thousand
annually, and the remaining large areas of unoccupied
land are in the more inaccessible sections of northern
Manchuria.

With the achievement of more complete control, there is by no means agreement in Japan on the direction that economic development should take in Manchuria. The army group is insistent that it shall not be left to the capitalists, and the capitalists are unwilling to venture any large sums unless they are permitted to retain the active supervision of their investment. At the present writing, the military is demanding that the economic development of Manchuria be placed completely under the control of the Japanese army in Kwantung with the exclusion of any supervision from civil authority in Japan proper.

In the months immediately following September, 1931, attention was centered upon the possibilities of Manchuria as a source of raw materials and power to relieve the handicaps of Japanese industry, and as a market for Japanese manufactures. To permit the unrestricted flow of commodities, the removal of all tariff barriers between Japan and the new state of Manchoukuo through the formation of an economic bloc was proposed. It was quickly perceived, however, that although such a policy might benefit some interests in Japan, it would mean the economic ruin of others equally important. The free import of the cheaper agricultural produce of Manchuria would lower the cost of living of the Japanese workers, but it would make even more precarious than at present the position of the Japanese farmers, a group comprising more than one half of the population. After the payment of transportation costs and the tariff, Fushun coal has undersold Japanese coal in Tokyo, and at the insistence of the Japanese mine operators, restrictions have been placed in the last few years upon the shipments from Manchuria. With the removal of the tariff, the pressure upon the Japanese mines would be increased, and more of them would be forced to close, thus throwing Japanese miners out of work, though Japanese industry, as a result of the imports, might receive cheaper coal. Japan is badly in need of iron ore, but the Manchurian ore is of such poor quality that it cannot be shipped economically over the long rail and water haul to Japan proper. It must be processed near the point of extraction. It is doubtful whether there is the basis in Manchuria for a really successful iron and steel industry, but the Japanese steel industry, so carefully built up by tariff and subsidies, fears the competition of the proposed Manchurian steel plant and opposes the free movement of its product to Japan. Because of objections in Japan, the economic bloc apparently has been abandoned. In its place there are being advanced rather vague plans for the development in Manchuria of only those economic activities that do not threaten to compete with the activities of Japan.

In trade, the strengthening of political control over Manchuria should result in gains to Japan. The example of Korea is perhaps pertinent. In the four years ending with 1930, Japan supplied 73 percent of the Korean imports, China 19 percent, and the rest of the world only 8 percent. Japanese exports to Manchuria, very largely in the form of supplies for the new construction program, have increased substantially in the last year, and imports from China proper have declined. Unless there is a departure from the policy of the Open Door, there can be no monopoly of the Manchurian market. With equal opportunity, British, German, Chinese, and Russian goods would continue to offer the competition that placed them in an important position in the market prior to 1931. Despite assertions to the contrary from Japan and Manchoukuo, there is every indication that the Open Door will exist only in name. Without any specific exclusion of other goods, many methods of keeping the trade in Japanese hands are available. Already, several European and American business concerns have closed their branches and withdrawn their representatives from Manchuria, or have indicated that they are about to do so as a result of Japanese discrimination.

In any attempt to measure the economic value of Manchuria to Japan, the claims of China cannot be ignored. Many sections of China are even more crowded than is Japan, and in recent years there has been a steady stream of migrants moving northward, particularly from Shantung and Hopei, in search of land for settlement. Manchuria is the most promising source of food to relieve the shortage that is always present in China proper. Industrialization has begun in China, and an increasing demand for raw materials, particularly iron ore, is certain. The Chinese deposits of ore are not large, and of the estimated actual and potential reserves, from 75 to 80 percent are situated in Manchuria. China cannot afford to acquiesce in this loss of territory. Armed resistance is out of the question for the present, but continued economic retaliation through the use of the boycott, resulting in losses to Japan which must be set against its gains in Manchuria, may be expected.

THE JAPANESE DILEMMA

The somewhat dubious outlook in Manchuria gives no assurance that Japan will recognize the futility of empire. It is quite probable that under the pressure of a growing population and the very serious deficiencies in resources Japan may attempt further expansion of territory through military conquest. Quite aside from the huge expenditures that would be involved in acquiring territory and in holding it, it may be reasoned from Western experience that such a policy would not improve substantially Japan's economic position. There is considerable doubt whether conquered markets and forced trade can ever be effective over any extended period, especially in the face of spreading industrialization.

The poverty of resources both in Japan proper and in territory under the control of Japan, indicated by the above brief inventory, has been one of the determining factors in the development of manufacturing. The industries that have flourished are either those that draw upon the limited list of raw materials produced within the country, or those that consume raw materials of small bulk and relatively high value obtainable from foreign countries without too great transport cost.

The leading manufacturing industry at the present time is the textile industry. It includes the reeling of raw silk, cotton-spinning, cotton-weaving, the weaving of silk and mixed cloth, the spinning and weaving of wool, hemp, flax, and other fibers, and the finishing of cloth. This group of industries employs about one half of all the factory workers and contributes some 45 percent of the total value of all manufactured goods and two thirds of the value of Japanese exports. The cocoons for the silk industry are the product of the steep slopes of Japan's mountainous interior. The raw cotton, raw wool, flax, ramie, and hemp are all sufficiently valuable to carry the cost of importation.

The heavier industries have experienced more serious difficulties. It has been noted that Japan possesses very small deposits of iron ore and inadequate reserves of coal of coking quality. Both are bulky raw materials costly to transport, and for the iron and steel industry of Japan both must be imported. Other nations lacking one or the other of these resources have built up an iron and steel industry, but no nation lacking both has ever been able to reach first rank in manufacturing. Considered essential partly because of its basic relationship to transportation and to all manufacturing, and partly because of its importance in maintaining a strong army and navy, the iron and steel industry, to a greater extent than any other Japanese industry, has received active support and encouragement from the government, but the achievements have been disappointing.

Liberal subsidies have been granted to the industry, and a high tariff has been placed upon imported products. The Japanese industry has had the added protection of the freight costs that must be paid on iron and steel goods imported from the distant European or American producing centers. The Japanese government has built a huge iron and steel plant at Yawata in northern Kyushu. It employs over half of the workers engaged in the primary refining of metals, and in 1928 it was estimated that it produced between 75 and 80 percent of the total pig-iron output of Japan and about 58 percent of the steel.

Despite all this assistance, the iron and steel industry is very small in comparison with that of other manufacturing countries. The pig-iron output is far below that of Belgium, or even of Luxemburg, although Japan has a population of 67 million, Belgium 8 million, and Luxemburg only 300,000. For the five-year period ending with 1932, the pig-iron output of Japan was 44 percent of that of Luxemburg and 31 percent of that of Belgium. In steel the comparison is a little more favorable, since the Japanese output of steel ingots and castings for the same period was 95 percent of the output of Luxemburg and 63 percent of that of Belgium. The Japanese iron and steel industry may be expected to expand to some extent. It will continue to depend upon government support for its existence, and it must draw upon foreign sources for its raw materials. It may assure self-sufficiency in the event of war, particularly with access to the low-grade ore deposits of Manchuria, and it will supply a large part of the demand in the domestic market protected by a high tariff and subsidies. On the other hand, Japanese industry and transportation will be handicapped by the necessity of purchasing equipment produced at costs higher than those prevailing in Western countries. There is no prospect of the eventual establishment of a primary iron and steel industry capable of competing in world markets.

Because of the scarcity of resources within the Empire, Japanese manufacturing from the beginning of the modern period has been dependent to a very large extent upon imports for its raw materials. The rapid growth of industry is reflected in the increase in the value of imports from an average of 31 million yen per year in the period just prior to 1880 to 1.8 billion yen for the five years ending with 1932. The most significant item in the import trade at present is raw cotton. From a minor position in the earlier years it has advanced both absolutely and relatively and now represents from 25 to 30 percent of the total import trade. There have been increases, though less spectacular, in the imports of other raw materials: raw wool, timber, petroleum, and pig iron. Raw materials and commodities intended for further manufacture now constitute 70 percent of the import trade. In the earlier years, manufactured goods were the most important group in the imports, but they now equal not more than 15 or 16 percent of the total.

Though raw materials have been vital to industrialization, their import has imposed upon the country the necessity of providing payment, and for Japan payment has meant mainly the export of commodities. Little Japanese capital is invested abroad, and there has been only limited development of such services as shipping and insurance so important in balancing the trade of Great Britain. Exports have expanded rapidly, but not in sufficient volume to keep pace with imports. Japan normally has an adverse balance in commodity trade, and it has been necessary to borrow abroad to pay for a part of the imports. Since 1895 exports have exceeded imports in only six years, four of them during the World War. It is because of the huge excess of imports that has been piling up in the last decade and because of the mounting burden of foreign debt that the expansion of trade is so essential to Japan at the present time.

Throughout all of the modern period, one item, raw

silk, has occupied the position of major importance. Since 1876 it has constituted from 35 to 40 percent of the value of all export trade. It is Japan's main dependence, and if its market should suddenly be destroyed, economic ruin would probably follow. Indicative of both the degree and the trend of Japanese industrialization has been the notable relative increase in the position of other textile products in the export trade. In the earlier years, cotton textiles, silk tissues, and clothing were the principal items of import. In the exports, they constituted less than 0.5 percent of the total. Today they have become insignificant in the import trade, and the group of textile products, including raw silk, cotton yarn and cloth, silk tissues and clothing, account for from 65 to 75 percent of the exports. As Japanese trade has developed, the exports have formed two major streams. Raw silk, a luxury product, has gone to the United States, and the textile staples, cotton especially, have gone to the countries of Asia. At present these two markets take about 80 percent of the export trade.

Efforts have been made to diversify both the list of exports and the markets, but it is not likely that any major change in the general character of Japanese trade will occur in the near future. It is in the textile industries that the most promising opportunities for industrial expansion are presented, and it is upon Japan's ability to market abroad its textile products that its future as an industrial nation depends. The United States possesses the high purchasing power necessary for the absorption of the raw silk, and the adjacent countries of Asia, with their crowded millions, all wearing cotton, are the natural market for the more staple textiles.

In the development of industry and trade, Japan has followed a course already marked out by the Western manufacturing nations, more especially by Great Britain. Raw materials have been imported, fabricated within the country, and then reëxported to pay for more raw materials. Despite the progress that has been made, however, there is little likelihood that Japan can attain even for the continent of Asia a position of importance comparable to that held by Great Britain in world trade in the eighteenth and nineteenth centuries. Japan possesses within its own territory few raw materials; Great Britain, though importing many requirements of industry, has had a number of resources, in particular excellent reserves of the two basic and bulky raw materials, coking coal and iron ore. There has been no shortage of power, and the iron and steel industry has been of major importance both for domestic consumption and for export.

Great Britain was the pioneer in the development of factory industry. In other countries, manufacturing continued to be carried on as a handicraft industry and Great Britain was able to enjoy all of the competitive advantages of the cheaper machine processes. As trade expanded, Great Britain entered virtually virgin markets all over the world, and for many years she was the only country sufficiently advanced industrially to supply the demand for manufactured goods. Other countries were still occupied with extractive industries and were not yet prepared for industrialization. Japan entered world trade more than a century later and has enjoyed no such monopoly. Few virgin markets remained, and as Japanese trade has expanded, it has been very largely through the displacing of the goods of the Western nations.

With the passing of time, many of the factors favoring the control of trade and industry by the West have disappeared or have been minimized, and certain economic assets of Japan have begun to function. The rôle of pioneer was of real advantage to Great Britain, but some of its disadvantages are beginning to accrue to British industries. Though British factories were the first, they are now old, and they contain much old machinery. There is a natural reluctance to discard it as long as it will operate, even when it is evident that newer types are more efficient. The factories of the more recently industrialized countries are able to install the latest machinery. In the factories of Japan there is much antiquated machinery purchased second hand abroad through a false economy or because of a scarcity of capital, but taken by and large, the equipment of the Japanese textile mills is newer than the equipment of the British mills, and the Japanese operators make the claim that their mills are more efficient.

One of Japan's greatest advantages for industrialization, long viewed with envy by Western manufacturers, is a dense population with a low standard of living that provides factory labor at low wages. It is true that much of this labor is unskilled and inefficient, and labor costs have been high despite low wages. With experience, efficiency has improved, and the introduction of the newer and more automatic machinery has made skill a less significant consideration. At the same time, there has been no compensating rise in wages, and labor costs are becoming lower and lower. It is an advantage that Japan should continue to enjoy, certainly in comparison with Occidental nations, since it is not likely that there will be any immediate advance in wages. In the last few years, they have declined. There is even the possibility that they may be pushed still lower in the next decade or so, when there will be from the present annual increase in population a net addition each year of some four hundred and fifty thousand or five hundred thousand to the number of individuals seeking employment.

For the further growth of Japanese trade, Asia holds out much greater promise than does America or any other region of the world. In the non-Asiatic countries, there is the handicap of distance and also of a culture quite foreign to Japan. Occidental tastes may be imitated, but in goods that respond frequently to dictates of style, it is difficult from so great a distance to keep pace with the changing demand. It has been a common experience of Japanese manufacturers, after sending representatives to study and report upon the current styles of the American markets, to find an entirely different fashion in vogue by the time the goods have been manufactured in Japan and shipped to the United States. It is partly for that reason that raw silk continues to be the principal item in the export trade with the Occident. It constitutes over 80 percent of the Japanese exports to the United States, Japan's leading customer. It is an export that may grow in importance, but it cannot be expected to expand as rapidly as might a more varied trade in staple manufactures. Japan already supplies most of the American demand, and shipments can be increased only through an increase in the American consumption of silk manufactures brought about by a more numerous population, a higher standard of living, or much lower prices.

In many of the Occidental countries, also, industries have been established to supply the demand for manufactures. It is difficult for Japanese goods to enter such markets, and their incursions are usually only temporary, for Japanese exporters have found repeatedly that if their competition becomes too successful there is immediate agitation for higher protective duties. With the present nationalistic tendencies in Europe and America, it is likely that such obstacles will be even more numerous and more formidable. Within the last few months there has been the demand for new or increased tariffs directed against Japanese goods in the United States, Great Britain, the Netherlands, Egypt, and in numerous colonial possessions of European powers.

The difficulties encountered in the Western countries have served to center the attention of Japan upon Asia. It is a market possessing great potentialities. In the eastern and southern portions of the mainland and in the adjacent islands, there live approximately one billion people or more than one half of the world's population. It is true that the purchasing power of this market is small. The great majority of the people are engaged in agriculture of a subsistence type that yields such meager returns that there is little surplus for the purchase of imported commodities. The limited transportation facilities hamper the shipment of goods into the interior, and manufactures are consumed chiefly in the coastal cities. The rural areas are still to a considerable degree self-supporting. They provide their own food requirements, and the necessary manufactured articles are produced in the small handicraft industries of the village. In 1929, the imports of China, with a population of probably 400 million, were only $820 million gold, and of India, with 350 million population, $1,173 million gold. For the same year, the Netherlands with a population of 8 million imported goods for consumption within the country to the value of $1,106 million.

It is reasonable to expect, however, that the purchasing power of this region will not remain at its present low level. Improvements in transportation are being introduced, and they will permit goods to penetrate deeper and deeper into the interior. It will also be possible for sections of the countries to specialize upon occupations for which they are best suited, looking to other areas to supply other needs. The passing of the present self-sufficiency will undoubtedly increase productivity, as it did in Japan in the years immediately following the opening of the country. Purchasing power will thus be expanded. It will also be increased by the spread of industrialization, giving to the people a greater earning power than is possible with their present dependence upon the land. It seems highly probable that Asia will experience in the next few decades a spectacular expansion in trade.

Low production costs, combined with proximity of position and a demand for the coarse, cheap type of goods that Japanese manufacturing is able to supply, have given to Japan a distinct advantage over Western nations in the Asia market and have favored the rapid penetration of Japanese trade. The portion of the exports of Japan going to China and to the other countries of the continent has increased from less than 25 percent in 1880 to over 40 percent in recent years. Not only has this trade been of increasing relative importance to Japan, but Japan has been supplying a larger and larger share of the Asiatic imports. The gains have been made at the expense of the Western countries that have occupied the leading position in Oriental trade for more than a century. For example, in the five-year period from 1906 to 1910, just after the conclusion of the Russo-Japanese War, Japan supplied approximately 18 percent of China's imports; in 1930 this had grown to 27 percent, and in some of the intervening years, especially during the World War, the Japanese share of the Chinese trade was even greater. Over the same spread of years, the British participation in the Chinese import trade declined from about 23 percent to 10 percent. Japan's most notable trade expansion has been in the products of its leading manufacturing industry, cotton spinning and weaving. In 1913 the China market obtained about 60 percent of its import of cotton piece goods from Great Britain, and 21 percent from Japan; in 1930, the most recent year not affected by the boycott, Japan supplied 76 percent and Great Britain only 15 percent. Japan has also made significant gains at the expense of Great Britain in British Malaya, the Netherlands East Indies, and British India. In more recent months, with the depreciation of the yen and under the necessity of finding new markets for goods excluded from China by the boycott, the increase of Japanese exports to southeast Asia and to British India has been greatly accelerated.

There is no desire to give the impression that Japan can achieve a monopoly of the Asia market. The United States and the other Occidental nations may be expected to share in the expansion of trade resulting from increased individual purchasing power, but opportunities will be restricted largely to heavy iron and steel goods, machinery, and other equipment for the new industrialization. In cotton textiles, the great staple of the trade and the prize of the eighteenth and nineteenth centuries, the advantages of Japan are too decided.

In the competition for the trade of Asia, Japan has had to meet the results of Western expansion and imperialism. Not only has it been necessary to break the established hold of European and American goods in the markets, but large areas of the continent are under the political control of Western nations. They are valued for their trade possibilities, and in India, Malaya, French Indo-China, and the Philippine Islands, tariffs give preference to the imports of the mother country and restrict the outsider. In only the Netherlands East Indies is there equality of opportunity.

Another obstacle to trade has been the conflict of Japanese political and economic interest in China. The importance of trade has been appreciated, and efforts have been made to encourage it, but the ambition to extend political control over territory or resources has repeatedly aroused bitter antagonism. China has resorted to the one effective weapon at its disposal, economic retaliation. Since 1915 there have been in

China seven major boycotts directed against Japanese goods. The present boycott began in the summer of 1931 with the massacre of the Chinese in Korea, but it did not become a significant movement until after the Manchurian incident in September. In the twenty-one months of the boycott ending with May, 1933, Japanese exports to China proper and Hong Kong declined by 213 million yen or by 47 percent in comparison with previous months. In time, the full force of the boycott tends to soften, but unquestionably Japanese trade in China would be much more important today if there had not been the interruption of these periods of hostility.

The urge to industrialize is spreading, and in more recent years it has been necessary for Japan to compete both with the older manufacturing countries and with new industries that are being established in some of its best markets, usually behind the protection of a tariff. A number of the countries of Asia, both sovereign states and dependencies, are giving active encouragement to manufacturing. China and India, in particular, possess advantages for industry in some respects superior to those of Japan. Both are crowded countries with a population pressing too heavily upon the land. Their standard of living is below that in Japan and their labor supply is larger and cheaper though it is as yet unskilled. Both countries grow cotton. China has one of the world's richest reserves of coal, and India has huge deposits of high-grade iron ore and a fair supply of coking coal. For both countries the potential domestic market is very large.

The greatest industrial development has taken place

in those industries upon which Japan has become most dependent, mainly cotton spinning and weaving. China has four million spindles in its mills, and in the larger cities there are numerous other factory industries. In India is located one of the largest iron and steel plants of Asia. Because of its excellent supplies of iron ore, it is able to produce pig iron at costs lower, probably, than the costs prevailing in any other country, but for steel manufacture labor is not sufficiently skilled or efficient, and costs are higher than in the European plants. In the Indian cotton mills there were in 1932 about 9.3 million spindles or about 1.7 million more than there were in Japan, though the Indian industry is much less efficient than the Japanese. Industrialization may even spread to the Netherlands East Indies, for it was proposed recently that spinning and weaving mills should be moved from the Netherlands to Java, primarily to meet the competition of Japanese goods.

To protect their new industries, the Asiatic countries are erecting tariff barriers. The movement toward tariffs in India, in so far as it has been encouraged from Great Britain, has been for the protection of a colonial market, but there has also been an insistence upon protection from within India as Japanese goods, especially textiles, have flooded the bazaars and seriously cut in upon the market of the Indian mills. The tariff increases have been general in their provision, but in practice they have been directed against Japanese goods, since the higher rates apply to kinds and grades of commodities supplied mainly by Japan. In March, 1933, the Indian tariff was increased from 30 percent *ad valorem* to 50 percent on silk and artificial silk piece goods, a type of cloth that has been shipped from Japan to India in rapidly increasing quantities. The rate of duty on cotton piece goods of non-British origin was raised recently to 75 percent, with the rate on British goods remaining at 25 percent. In April of this year, notice was given by the Indian government through the British Foreign Office of the abrogation of the Indo-Japanese trade agreement, an action presaging still further increases in the Indian duties on Japanese goods through the application of a dumping law enacted at the same time.

The abrogation of the trade treaty is an expression of a growing antagonism in the Indian market, as Japanese exporters, aided by the depreciated yen, have attempted through an aggressive sales policy and drastic price-cutting to make good their losses in China due to the boycott. Feeling has been bitter, and charges of dumping have been made. The Japanese, though admitting the advantages of the depreciated yen, deny that there has been dumping and insist that their success in the Indian market has been due mainly to the superior efficiency of their cotton mills. The announcement of the abrogation of the treaty has been received in Japan with considerable alarm since the trade with India has increased very substantially in importance in the last few years. In 1927, 8.4 percent of Japan's total exports were sent to India; in 1932 the ratio had increased to 13.7 percent. It has been charged that the action of the Indian government was dictated by the Lancashire cotton interests, and a part of the popular antagonism that has been displayed toward America in recent months has been diverted substantially the duties on those items that had been favored by the treaty. The action of China was in part political in retaliation for Japanese activities in Manchuria, but it undoubtedly was inspired also by the desire to encourage and protect Chinese manufacturing industries.

The necessity of competing with the industrialization of the other Oriental countries presents a serious problem to Japan and to the Japanese workers. With a disadvantage in raw materials and with a higher wage level, there will be a tendency to bring pressure upon labor to reduce production costs and thus assume much of the burden of competition. A lowering rather than a raising of the Japanese standard of living may conceivably result.

There is evident in Japan a growing feeling that the concentration of the control of capital in a few hands is responsible for the difficulties of the country. One expression of that feeling has been the physical attacks upon the industrialists and upon the political leaders who are considered to be closely allied with them. There have been demands for a much greater degree of public control over industry and commerce, extending to some form of fascism or state capitalism. Though the results attained so far have been meager, many plans for economic reorganization have been proposed under the guise either of rationalization or of combinations and mergers with state participation. That the agitation is being taken seriously by capital has been indicated by large donations for the public welfare made by several of the powerful companies, and by the announcement of the reorganization of one of those companies, previously a closed family concern, to permit a greater degree of participation by the public.

In the attacks upon capital, there would seem to be some confusion of cause and effect. Japan's present economic position can scarcely be attributed to the accumulation of capital in a few hands. The concentration is itself one of the results of the same conditions that have produced the difficulties of today. When the country was first opened to the world and attention was turned to manufacturing industry, there was a scarcity of capital, partly because commercial activities had been so unimportant and partly because the poverty of the country did not provide any great surplus. Both locally and nationally Japan was on a subsistence basis. Some relatively large financial transactions were carried on in connection with the government, and they were placed in the hands of a few favored families. With the new demand for capital, it was necessary for the government either to supply it through borrowing abroad or to turn to those same families. In a richer country, there undoubtedly would have occurred in time the rise of a numerous capitalistic class. In Japan, however, though there are thousands of small industrial enterprises, the opportunities for the small man have been too limited. The powerful have succeeded under the changed economic system, and the concentration of control has been perpetuated.

The scarcity of capital has always been a handicap to Japanese industry. High interest charges have hampered expansion and have discouraged the introduction of new machinery and equipment. Concentrated control, however, has given a centralized direc-

SOVIET SIBERIA

SOVIET SIBERIA
Joseph Barnes

THERE are two symptoms of fever in Siberia today:
machines and men. At any of the stations or on any
siding along the Trans-Siberian Railway east of the
Urals you can see them: shiny new Buicks lined up on
a ribbon of muddy road, flat cars with the forms of
harvesters and combines sharply outlined against the
sky, long trains of peasant families, laden with their
bedding and their samovars, moving east to open a
new continent. Backed by the old pressure of crowded
peoples upon unopened land and by the new pressures
of the Soviet state, this machinery and these people
are moving through the great Eurasian plain towards
the Pacific. They represent the new economic power
and the revolutionary ideas which have taken form in
Russia since 1917, impinging on the outer world to the
east through Siberia. They carry with them the promise
or the threat of sudden and violent change in the
human geography of the whole Pacific basin.

This is no new movement. The plains of the Ukraine and the valley of the Volga from which these settlers come have long been overcrowded, in terms of the possibility of working a living from the soil with the tools of primitive agriculture. Even the remorseless drive of the Bolsheviks which impels these migrants eastward is no new phenomenon to Russia. In 1580, an enterprising Cossack named Yermak crossed into Siberia with a little band of outlaws like himself, to begin the history of Russia in Asia. Three hundred and fifty years later, bands of *kulaks*, well-to-do peasants dispossessed and outlawed by the Bolshevik campaign to socialize the land as the Cossacks were outlawed by the land policy of the Czars, are following in his footsteps. The new settlers do not have to fight their way, except against cold and swamp and an empty, lonely land, the same stubborn enemies today as in the sixteenth century.

The form and the meaning of this migration, however, have completely altered. The tall, hard-riding Cossacks (whose red beards have gone into the Chinese language as the word for bandits) would have little in common with the quiet peasants of today, en route to work in a new coal mine or on a wheat farm being shaped out of the central Asian steppe-land. The first movement had furs and loot and adventure as its goals; the second has the more prosaic lure of new towns, factories, irrigated cotton fields. The force behind the eastward thrust of the old empire, which carried its steel rails to the Pacific, through Manchuria and to the frontiers of China in central Asia, was the desire for new lands, new ports, new riches. Since 1917 this force has turned inward. Soviet imperialism, if the phrase may be used at all, is no less urgent or remorseless than its Romanov prototype, but it is intensive instead of extensive, it seeks not new lands but new uses for old lands, and in its machines and men it carries with it the roots of a new civilization.

The pressure of population which underlay the imperial expansion into Siberia can be understood only in terms of the living economy of European Russia. Even in the first years of the twentieth century, when new industrial construction was beginning to absorb peasants into the cities, the inadequacy of Russia's farming lands, under the prevailing system of ownership, was one of the salient features of the old régime. Almost medieval farming methods, with small holdings and primitive tools, made the pressure more intense.

At the same time, there was little possibility of alleviating it, even in Asia. Large sections of Siberia lie either within the Arctic circle, where frost is king, or south of the rainfall line, which means to the wheat farmer the peril of drought. The fertile lands through which the railroad runs were not open lands for colonization. Like the unused lands of China, they were already held by landlords, officials, and speculators. Outside these lands, an individual settler was inevitably not so much a pioneer as a gambler. If he could manage to weather one bad harvest in four, he was still little better off than in the district he had left. If drought came once in two or three years, he was finished.

Thus the Urals remained a frontier without glamour. Officials sent to Siberia considered themselves demoted, and the population was made up of criminals, political exiles, mine and railroad workers, and a growing class of independent farmers. Even in 1907, when more than six hundred and fifty thousand colonists made the long journey to the Russian New World, the natural increase of the peasant population in European Russia was not balanced. The large and growing movement of colonists back to the crowded villages which they had left, which reached seventy-six thousand in 1910, is evidence of the difficulties and disappointments which these settlers found in Siberia. The construction of the Trans-Siberian Railway, at the turn of the century, provided access to world markets for Siberian wheat, butter, and lumber, but with no growing local markets and with inadequate means of transport and distribution, economic development proceeded slowly in the years before the war.

During this period, the frontiers of Asiatic Russia, both political and economic, were being steadily extended. With the borrowed power of French finance, tied into the pattern of European politics, imperial Russia edged closer and closer to India, to China, and to the Pacific. To the Western world, Russia seemed destined to dominate the continent of Asia, even after the defeat by Japan in 1904–05.

The national policy of imperial Russia before the World War was shaped along this line. It was the traditional pattern of military empire. A warm-water port, political control over those portions of China's periphery which Japan could be induced to share, a modern railroad financed by the savings of French peasants—these seemed to a statesman like Witte the answers to Russia's age-old problems. They would increase prestige in the West, and at the same time provide a safety valve against the growing unrest at home. A rapidly growing foreign debt demanded exports, and Siberia was thought to be the treasure house of the world. Pinioned as so often before in its history between Asia and Europe, Russia in the first decades of this century turned to Asia for a way out.

The attempt was not to succeed. Western forces and ideas had penetrated too deeply; the imperial structure was hopelessly undermined. The collapse came in 1917, when the hunger of the Russian people for bread and land and peace demolished the center of this far-stretched empire. At the same moment, its sections fell apart. The links on which it had been built were weak, and there was no force but the railroad which could begin to hold it together. When the root of imperial autocracy had been cut in St. Petersburg and Moscow, the granite buildings of officials in northern Manchuria and the army garrisons in Turkistan were seen to have no roots at all. There were Russian settlers, but few of them had any close relations to the land from which they had fled or been driven in long convict trains. And these were surrounded by Mongols, Turqi, Kazaks, and Uzbeks, tribes of herdsmen and hunters who had been defeated by Russians and then exploited by them for generations past. Only the railroad remained, a single-tracked communication tying Siberia to European Russia.

Along this railroad, for nearly five years, the revolution for bread, land, and peace was the principal commodity transported. White armies and Red Guard bands were carried, together with munitions and occasional supplies of food and clothing, but even this freight was insignificant compared to the ideas which moved from Moscow and St. Petersburg eastward to the Pacific. Except for the railroad itself, and a few thin threads of tradition in pockets of old Russian settlement, these ideas are the only elements of cohesion which today bind Siberia to Russia within the Soviet Union. They were planted wide and deep by the civil war; famine and hardship have strengthened them since then. It is their driving power which is threatening now to change the face of Siberia and to reshape the balance of power in the Pacific.

It is a curious and bitter irony that the Allied campaign in Siberia should have been one of the chief factors in establishing the power of the Bolsheviks in this region. The motives of the countries which sent expeditionary forces, money, and arms to Siberia are by no means clear. Whether it was to aid the Czech legions, who wished to return home around the world and were quite capable of doing so unaided, to reconstitute an eastern front against Germany, which seems today a plan almost too fantastic for belief, or to take advantage of a troubled situation in the hope of large-scale plunder and concessions when the war had ended, as the Bolsheviks charge, the results were unequivocal.

The stupidity and ineptitude of White leaders was reinforced by all the flavor of foreign invasion. Thanks to intelligent military leadership, the record of the American expeditionary force was relatively clear. The United States contributed to the strength of Bolshevism only by its destroyers in the harbor at Vladivostok and its soldiers policing the railroad lines. Others of the Allies were not so scrupulous. Kolchak, Horvath, Semenov, and a motley group of other Whites, ranging from incapable military figureheads to fanatic adventurers, were equipped and financed by powers with a large stake in the stemming of Bolshevism. With this foreign help, these remnants of a dead aristocracy tried for over four years to rally the people of Siberia to a cause which had no chance of life. By their blunders, and by the foreign intervention which they used, they served only to drive the farmers of Siberia into the arms of Lenin's party.

Not until 1922 did the last of the Japanese regiments embark from Vladivostok. By this time, the chances of a moderate democratic government in Siberia, which had been good at the outbreak of the revolution, had completely disappeared. The Far Eastern Republic, set up as a buffer state to negotiate with foreign countries, was ready to merge its identity in the Union of Socialist Soviet Republics. The White Guard detachments had been liquidated or driven across the frontier into Mongolia or China. Traffic on the railroad was restored to a point a little nearer normal. Men, a few machines, and the first thin trickle of goods began again to come from Moscow. The farmers and workers of Siberia, always more independent and less desperate than those west of the Urals, accepted communism with bitter memories of the civil war and intervention still fresh in their minds, with longing for peace and stability and a chance to grow their crops again.

The liberal and democratic leaders who emerged during the early years had emigrated or disappeared.

In their places came younger and less educated men, who were not afraid of power. Some of these, like Sukhanov, were from the upper classes; more of them, men like Nikiferov and Melnikov, were from the "dark people." Siberia's imports of revolutionaries were during these years heavier than its exports. Utkin and Jordan came from Australia, Antonov from Naples, Krasnoschekoff and Shatov from the United States. Trained in communist doctrine either in Moscow or in underground groups abroad, these men set out to make a Soviet Siberia.

From Moscow, directly after Lenin came to power, help was forthcoming in the form of men, goods, and money. After the first flurry of revolution in western Europe had died out, when the Bolshevik leaders were preparing to dig themselves in for a long siege by a hostile world, Siberia loomed large on the map of Russia. It was not new provinces, however, or international railroad politics, or the lust for colonies in China that turned the Soviet face eastward. It was rather the need for raw materials, for men, for empty land.

In the main, this need was part and parcel of the communist experiment. The leaders of the 1917 revolution had deliberately unloosed expansive forces of tremendous potential strength. The entire area of the old Russian Empire was not too big a field for them to work in. In their nature these forces were intensive and not extensive. They involved violent reshaping of internal social and economic boundaries rather than of external political boundaries. The population pressure in the crowded plains of Russia, which had led Witte to seek new wheat lands in Manchuria, the Bolsheviks plan to relieve by state farms and collectivization. By rational control, they believe, it will be possible to turn new areas of western Siberia into grain-growing farms, accumulating reserves from the good harvests to tide over the years when not enough rain falls in this region. Most important of all, by industrializing Russia, these leaders have expected to use this population pressure to produce, not wars and famine, but man power for the manufacture of goods. All these ends, however, require large space and a free hand, both of which Siberia could supply.

Another reason for Siberia's importance to the development of the Soviet Union, especially urgent in the early years, was the fear of war. At one time during the revolution, Lenin was prepared to move the government east of the Urals if necessary, and he wrote then that one of the first tasks after peace had been won would be to establish a heavy industrial base in Siberia. During the civil wars, the Bolshevik leaders had learned that with oil in the Caucasus, coal and iron in the Don Valley, and a steel industry in the southern and western provinces, the sinews of national strength lay on their most vulnerable periphery. At no time since then have these leaders ever lost their fear of war. It is only natural that they should have strained every effort to create in the geographical security of Siberia a base of coal, iron, steel, and wheat on which they could fall back in times of military emergency.

The so-called Ural-Siberian metallurgical base has today taken shape as the corner stone of this plan. Halfway across the Ural Mountains, at Magnitogorsk, there is a city of 230,000 population where six years ago there was only a small village. Farther east in Siberia, at Kuzbass in the foothills of the Altai Mountains, another similar city is being built. At the first there are iron-ore reserves, while Russia's greatest deposits of coking coal are located at the second. With the help of American and German consultants, with a capital investment which eats up annually a frightening proportion of the national income of Soviet Russia, complete metallurgical plants are being built at both these places. When both are completed, they are expected to rank the Soviet Union second only to the United States as a producer of iron and steel.

Stories of this development have reached every village in the Soviet Union, where it has become the symbol of the Five-Year Plan and of the drive for industrialization. At the same time, these stories have reached the Pacific and other Far Eastern countries, where the new industrial plants are regarded as the threatening spearhead of an imperialism advancing eastward. Until all the furnaces have been blown in and the planned production of steel rails has been transferred from paper to the roadbeds of new railways, the reaction of the Russians must retain that quality of emotional enthusiasm which has stamped itself on so much of the Soviet experiment. The fears of other Pacific powers, however, that the new industrial base with its fringe of heavy machine factories represents a direct threat, either commercially or in a military sense, to the peace of the Pacific, have grown either from ulterior political motives or from that miasmic fog of misunderstanding and distrust with which the Soviet Union has been cloaked for the outside world since 1917.

The new factories are placed in an unopened wilderness. One has only to ride for long days through the endless waste spaces of the railroad belt which cuts across Siberia to realize that the steel production of the whole world could be poured into this continent for many years before any limit could even be guessed at. For reasons of defense, Soviet leaders are glad to have a base protected from the possibility of even air attack. Only a very long-term offensive military plan would call for industrial investments so far removed from Russia's frontiers. The problem of transporting coal and ore each way between Kuzbass and Magnitogorsk, a distance of 1,500 miles at present and 900 miles when a new railroad has been completed, presents difficulties which may strain even the subtleties of Soviet bookkeeping before steel can be exported except at a ruinous loss. To export coal, it has been estimated by American engineers, would require a consumption of three tons to carry every ton to a port of loading. And most important of all is the clear domestic urgency of this development. The Ural-Siberian base may change the balance of industrial power on the Pacific in a period of generations, as Gary, Indiana, has already helped to do. No more than Gary, however, is it an offensive threat to Japan or China or the peace of the Pacific.

Around this new base the first Five-Year Plan has already constructed a network of heavy factories. At Sverdlovsk, at Cheliabinsk, at Novosibirsk, there are tractor and locomotive factories, chemical plants and machine-building establishments. Siberia is comparatively rich in non-ferrous metals, and its lumber resources are the largest in the world. Its reserves of iron ore and coal have never been thoroughly investigated. Official Soviet estimates require undoubtedly a certain discount, and it is doubtful whether new discoveries will ever bulk large enough to make Siberia in any sense a rival to the great iron and coal centers of the North Atlantic basin. There is little reason to doubt, however, that the raw materials exist for a substantial development over what now prevails.

With every year, the planners of the Soviet Union have pushed the industrial center of the country farther eastward, until cracking plants for petroleum production are now on the shore of the Pacific, and the coal mines are being worked on a larger and larger scale on the island of Sakhalin. The line of development has so far been principally along the railroad, as was the case under the Czars, and the great new cities of Siberia are railroad cities. The intensive character of the new eastward thrust, however, directed primarily at the creation of a new society and a new economy within Russia, has made it spill over into the deserts of central Asia and Turkistan and into the frozen tundra of the Arctic north. In central Asia an independent cotton supply is being worked for, with irrigation developments turning the rivers of Tamerlane backward, and textile looms being set up in the shadows of Samarkand. Copper reserves, in which the Soviet Union is deficient, have been found near Lake Balkash. They are reported to be extensive. The great rivers of Siberia, hitherto useless as means of transport because they empty into the Arctic basin, play also a large part in Soviet plans. With ice-breakers, aërial surveys,

[98]

and competent management, it is at present hoped to open the Arctic route between Europe and Asia, a feat performed for the first time in a single season by a Soviet experimental ship in 1933. If this should prove to be feasible, it would open to exploitation by far the greater part of Siberia, which now lies protected by the intense cold from all but wandering tribes and occasional expeditions looking for gold or furs.

The Ural Mountains divide Siberia from European Russia only on the map. They are not high mountains, but rather low hills which stand out in the middle of the Eurasian plain. More formidable than mountains, the distance which separates Siberia from the heart of the Soviet Union presents a difficult problem. Great in actual mileage, it is enormous if measured in time or in the difficulty of transporting goods across it. The development of transport and communications is therefore of vital importance in the eastward orientation of Russia toward Asia and the Pacific.

The heritage of railroads left by the imperial régime was a potent agent in spreading the revolution across Siberia. Its adequacy for the task of reconstruction and industrialization is less apparent. The Trans-Siberian Railway, which spans the continent through its most fertile and prosperous belt, reaches Vladivostok and Pacific Ocean commerce by connection with the Chinese Eastern Railway, which cuts through northern Manchuria. The melodramatic history of this latter railroad, as well as its imperialistic taint, have always made the Soviet Union a little uneasy, and there are many reasons why its sale, or even its surrender, to Japan or the new state of Manchoukuo would bring a feeling of relief at Moscow. The alternative route to Vladivostok is by way of the Ussuri line, a road 600 kilometers longer which skirts the northern tip of Manchuria along the valley of the Amur River. Both military and commercial considerations show this line to be notably deficient when compared to the Chinese Eastern. In the long run, if Siberian industrialization accomplishes the results which Soviet planners expect, a shorter route to a warm-water port may be essential. The question will remain a constant irritant to Soviet-Japanese relations as long as the Soviet Union retains its financial interest in the line. The desire for peace within the U.S.S.R. is so imperative, however, that even the deficiencies of the longer Ussuri route are likely to be cheerfully overlooked.

Since 1922, railroad construction in Siberia has been pushed. The principal link has been the old line between Sverdlovsk in the Urals, and Novosibirsk, the capital city of Siberia. This is the line which links the two units of the new metal base, and it is destined inevitably to be the main artery of the new region. Other sections of the Trans-Siberian line have been double-tracked, and feeder lines are being built to tap mines and farm lands lying at some distance from the railroad.

The most spectacular construction has been the Turk-Sib Railroad. This line was surveyed by engineers before the war but constructed by the Soviets under the dynamic leadership of Bill Shatov, a former anarchist who left Russia when a boy to grow up in American mining towns and jails. It connects the great plains of central Asia, which by irrigation are planned to grow cotton, rubber substitutes, tea, and other semi-tropical produce, to the wheat and lumber of Siberia. Releasing the former area from the necessity of growing subsistence crops and enabling it to concentrate on production which the Soviet Union badly needs, it has at the same time opened a new market for Siberia's goods and a new route to the Caucasus and to Europe. This road is already in operation. Copper plants and textile mills are being built along it. The great textile mills of Moscow, which were built and developed on American cotton, now send annual expeditions of their workers into the heart of Asia at harvest time to help in the construction of a new and independent raw material base.

Second only to the Ural-Siberian industrial base, this Turk-Sib Railroad has been regarded in the East as a portent of the growing menace of Soviet imperialism. It flanks for a thousand miles the western borders of Mongolia and Chinese Eastern Turkistan. The Russians have not hesitated to publish their plans for branch railroads, none of which has yet been built, which will tap the produce of these areas. Even now the bulk of the foreign trade of both Mongolia and Chinese Eastern Turkistan travels by caravans or by motor truck to the Turk-Sib or the Trans-Siberian railroads. From Kashgar, the capital city of Sinkiang or Chinese Eastern Turkistan, to Peiping, in China, by direct route requires seventy days of tedious travel. By the Turk-Sib, it can be accomplished in thirteen days. This is an economic factor of large potential importance. These peripheral provinces of China, because of it, have gravitated into a Russian influence stronger probably than any which was produced before the war by Russian money or diplomatic promises.

Soviet leaders have not attempted to disguise the importance of this factor, although they have insisted that it constitutes a new and special kind of influence which should not be termed imperialism. They have pointed out the political importance to themselves of the whole area of central Asia. The proletarian revolution and the dictatorship of the workers which it has produced in Russia had real roots, it may be argued, only in the large cities of European Russia. They have been transplanted even to the Russian countryside only by violence, long effort, and shrewd maneuvering. How much less indigenous the revolution was to the deserts of central Asia need not be explained. Wandering tribesmen, cattle herders, and hunters, these descendants of Tamerlane the Magnificent, like their neighbors in Persia, Afghanistan, and China, presented to the Bolsheviks a problem in revolutionary technique which had no parallels in the experience of western Europe or of Russia.

They have not hesitated to admit this non-indigenous character of the revolution in central Asia, and until 1930 foreigners were not allowed to travel in these regions. The whole area has been made a sort of experimental field for revolutionary technique among Asiatic peoples. There can be no general agreement as to the degree of success which has so far been achieved. It seems true that disproportionately large capital investments have been made in these regions, partly because of the Soviet Union's real need for the economic products of warm districts—such as cotton, silk, and rubber—and partly because of the political importance of a region contiguous to Mongolia, Sinkiang, Persia, Afghanistan, and the Northwest Provinces of India. There is a very large degree of racial mixture overlapping these political boundaries. Nomadic cattle-breeders and Persian and Afghan traders have operated, remarkably enough, across the frontiers here without a break from 1917 to the present time. This breach in the Soviet foreign trade monopoly is allowed by the Soviet government, partly as a concession to local feeling, and partly as a remarkable method of political propaganda. Industrial communism is still a strange thing to these peoples, whose historical development is being telescoped through a half-dozen centuries in a couple of decades. Local revolts are still by no means impossible. The Turk-Sib Railroad, however, and the irrigation projects and textile mills which it brings with it, have given the Bolsheviks a lever against the traditions and resistances of Asiatic peoples, both those within the Soviet Union and those outside it, which is of large potential importance to the continent of Asia.

With industrial plants and with communications tying them to each other and to the rest of the Soviet Union, Siberia will still need men if it is to achieve the position in the Pacific which the leaders of the Russian Revolution have planned for it. It will still need leaders, men who are capable of carrying out these plans, and it will need population—workers, farmers, and consumers—to build the new country.

Both of these problems have proved to be among the most difficult which Siberia has had to face. The dearth of technicians, of trained men, capable of the skilled work which industrial construction requires, lies heavy over the whole face of Russia. Nowhere is it more acute than in Siberia, where bad living conditions, solitude, and a punishing climate provide no easy incentives. No real answer can be said to have been found as yet. The attempt has been to train a new generation of skilled engineers, doctors, teachers, and scientists from the ranks of the workers. This is at best a slow job. The number of qualified party workers stationed at lonely posts in the Far East is constantly growing. Behind them there is a cumulative social sentiment, which is something new in Russia, looking to Siberia as a land of promise and hope, and making work there, for large numbers of young men and women, at the same time a gesture of daring and adventure. Living conditions, and particularly the cultural perquisites of life which have in the past been so lacking in Russia outside of a few large cities, are being improved. The task ahead, however, is still colossal.

Transplanting people in bulk to the new areas has also been a knotty problem. Opening new lands for cultivation in Siberia is a task requiring organization, capital investment, and machinery. Many of them require drainage or irrigation, or are located in semi-arid regions where occasional crop failures must be expected and reserves set up against them. The nature of agriculture and of industry in this area, also, requires a large measure of organization, since it is being planned in careful integration with existing resources elsewhere. Transport and markets come to have, under such carefully integrated plans, an overwhelming significance.

Cattle-breeding and dairy-farming, which are particularly important in western Siberia, can be profitably engaged in only on a rather large scale under local conditions. All these factors make the pioneer, as he was known in the United States or even in Siberia before the war, an anachronism.

In his place, the Soviet planners have realized, there must be a careful and systematic migration of men equipped with tools to master their new physical environment. Anyone who has seen the long trains of box cars in Siberia filled with miserable peasants, their chickens, and their furniture, being shunted from siding to siding across the continent, has reason to doubt whether these careful plans are executed with any degree of precision. Against the background of the conditions from which these peasants move, however, and of the traditional methods of Asiatic migration, even this crude procedure shows some advance.

A special problem which Siberia has yet to face is the assimilation back into normal life of large groups of semi-outlawed individuals. Under the former régime, this assimilation never took place, and only the revolution erased legal and civil differences between former exiles and their fellow citizens. The Soviet government is sending exiles in numbers which must approach, if they do not exceed, the totals sent by the courts of the Czars. Most of them are *kulaks*, peasants who have openly resisted the collectivization campaign. The procedure by which their goods are confiscated and their families transported to lumber camps in the north or to new farms in the Siberian plains is more arbitrary than before the war. Whole villages in the south of

Russia have been moved in this manner. In their new homes, they are given a certain freedom, and the Bolsheviks have been too eager for man power to leave them, like the pre-war exiles, with no functional relationship to their environment. For the most part they are used on new construction, in lumber camps, and on state farms. With the children and the younger generation, the Soviet leaders expect to accomplish the task of assimilation, so that these may become the backbone of the proletariat of the new Siberia. With the older generation, even the Bolsheviks admit, the tragedy of broken families, disrupted homes, and human bitterness has few redeeming features.

The importance of these factories, railroads, and new people lies still in the future. How far the second Five-Year Plan may succeed in transferring it to the present depends on peace, the slow and tortuous learning of new skills and a new way of life by millions of people, and on the desperate abstinence which is required by any capital accumulation from national income alone. For the present, Siberia remains a continent of soil, still in the process of being broken into civilization by agriculture, by the growing of food.

In the future, too, agriculture will play a predominant part in the life of Siberia. Even without ready access to warm-water ports, the centralized control of national economy in the Soviet Union will make it possible to develop Siberia as a granary for the entire country, thus releasing the products of the northern Caucasus and of the Ukraine for export purposes. This is the basis of the present plans. The cotton, rubber substitutes, tea, and silk of central Asia are designed to supplant costly imports. The wheat, rye, and flax of western Siberia are grown for a home market, in order to permit concentration in other localities on cultivation of other crops or on production for export. The dairy farming and meat production of the northern and eastern ports of Siberia are expected to account for the bulk of the national supply of these products.

How far the present agricultural production of Siberia may be extended or increased is a question of some uncertainty. Covering over five million square miles, an area nearly twice that of the United States, Siberia would seem to have infinite possibilities of increased production. Aside from fishing and furs, however, little more than a quarter of this vast territory appears at present to be adaptable to any form of economic exploitation. The vast stretches of the Arctic north, where the frost does not leave the ground even in the summer, merge into the forest belts, a broad zone of coniferous trees stretching all the way to the Pacific. Below this is the wheat and agricultural belt, where the railway runs, which fades out to the south into steppe and desert land. Extension of the area under cultivation at present must probably come in this last section. How far large-scale farming, irrigation, improved methods of seed selection, and deliberate accumulation of reserves against drought will prove to be effective against the menace of inadequate rainfall, only longer experience will tell.

The problem of reclaiming semi-arid soils in the south, or of introducing some form of agriculture in the frozen tundra of the north, is secondary in the Soviet Union today. Of more urgent importance is the necessity of expanding production by means of increased yields per acre and more effective disposition of the goods produced. Along this line there is little doubt that much progress could be made. Railroads and motor roads, irrigation and improved farming methods, agricultural machinery and better seed selection could work wonders in the farms of Siberia. Particularly in the dairy and cattle-breeding sections, present methods of husbandry differ only very slightly from those practised centuries ago on these same plains by the nomad ancestors of present tribesmen. The principal energy of Soviet reconstruction in Siberia at the present time is being directed at this problem. Again, it is too early to say whether state and collective farms of large size, serviced by tractor stations, designed to substitute a worker's collective psychology for the traditional way of life of Asiatic farmers, provide the answer. It is important to realize, however, that if in any significant measure they should succeed, it would be an answer not only to the problems of Siberia's development, but to many of the questions which are being asked in other Asiatic lands today.

A Bolshevik Siberia has an importance to the Pacific, and to all the nations which have interests there, which does not depend upon the length of its Pacific coast line. Now that the revolution itself in Russia has faded into the problem of reconstruction, it has become apparent that a new set of ideas and values has been established, which no blockade can completely embargo. The communist plan for Siberian development is more, essentially, than a series of blueprints for factories, railroads, new schools, and reorganized agriculture. It is a way of life, a social revolution in accepted standards and relationships. As such it has meaning to the people of Siberia and to those of China, to the workers of Japan and of the United States. As the economic development of this new Pacific territory proceeds, these ideas will impinge with increasing sharpness on the lives of other peoples of the Pacific.

It has become customary to regard this centrifugal influence of the Soviet Union on the world, and especially on the Far East, as exclusively a matter of skillful propaganda, directed by somewhat sinister underworld agents of the Third International. Similarly, after the French Revolution, liberty, equality, and fraternity were thought by large sections of Europe to be little more than the salesmen's samples of corrupt French agents engaged in subversive activities. Both explanations are too easy. If the agents of the Third International could justifiably be credited with the unrest and sedition which at present fill the Pacific area, and particularly the Far East, it would be an achievement to dwarf the Five-Year Plan.

The spreading influence of communism in the Pacific has been far more closely related to the troubles of that area. Soviet goods and ships, travelers and tourists, magazines and newspapers have been the carriers of ideas, but they have taken root only where something in local conditions has created a soil favorable to them. It has required some years for Soviet Russia itself to discover that revolutions are not carried in suitcases. It is a truth which the rest of the world has yet to learn.

Immediately after 1917, the leaders of the Russian Revolution confidently expected a wave of revolutionary outbreaks which would bring other European countries under some form of proletarian dictatorship. Whether they underestimated the vitality of capitalism or simply guessed the time inaccurately, it is impossible to say. After their early disillusionment, however, the Third International turned to the East. The Leninist theory of imperialism, which allies the workers of industrial countries with the exploited natives of colonial lands, provided a theoretical basis for work in India, China, and other Asiatic countries. The sudden and violent industrialization of Japan had created social and economic conditions in that country which lent themselves peculiarly to a Marxist analysis, and there were many in Moscow who predicted a revolution in that country. Finally, the post-war prosperity seemed to indicate the beginning of a new era of imperialist competition for raw materials and markets which would accelerate the process that the leaders of the Third International saw as leading inevitably to complete collapse.

In practical terms, the policy pursued by the Third International has come to be known as the United Front. In the East this meant for the most part a temporary coalition with bourgeois elements who were working for national emancipation from imperialist oppression. In China, Sun Yat-sen was wrestling with the problems of the Kuomintang, attempting to forge from its disparate elements a working tool for the achievement of national freedom. In Michael Borodin, a legendary revolutionary character with a background of experience in three continents and with a personality which fitted well into the Chinese scene, Moscow found perhaps the ideal individual to offer and deliver its support to this national movement. From the date of his arrival in Canton in September, 1923, the Soviet Union was in fact, if not by diplomatic recognition, deeply involved in the Chinese struggle.

Dispute still rages over the reasons for the temporary success and subsequent failure of this struggle. It is clear that Borodin and his staff of Russian-trained revolutionists brought to China a discipline, a working method, and a doctrinal basis which were not to be found in the Kuomintang, and which have left their imprint on parts of China even today. It is equally clear that the social and class basis of the Nationalist movement in China was too scattered and too inchoate to hold together, and that the final collapse in 1927, when Borodin retired across the Gobi Desert in an old Dodge touring car, was fated from the very beginning of his adventure. The National government which emerged from the wreckage of the 1925–27 revolution bears little sign of its early Soviet association, but elsewhere in China, and especially in the so-called communist districts of central China, there are nuclei of uncertain future. The conditions under which these Soviet districts have developed and grown suggest that they represent more a bitter agrarian revolt against the oppression of usurious landlords and incompetent government than any proletarian or communist revolution. At the same time, much of the influence left behind by Borodin has clung to these districts, and any alliance which they could form with the working proletariat of

Hankow or Shanghai might have enormous importance for the future of China.

In Japan, the influence of the Third International has been less spectacular and even less clear. While the United Front policy was being followed, no progress was made in Japan except among student groups. Since 1928, when, after the collapse of the Chinese experiment and of the General Strike in England, the Third International discarded the United Front with other parties, the communist movement in Japan has gone underground. Whether the present spread of Fascist ideas has caught up the malcontents or whether there is still a future for a Japanese communist party, few would dare to predict. So long as there are discontent and struggle within the country, the pressure of the government and the police to stamp out communists will indicate at least their conviction of its urgent menace.

In other countries of Asia, the technique of the Soviets has also varied. In none of these has it been more interesting, nor perhaps more significant, than in Outer Mongolia. Most remote of all the provinces of China from its central government, separated from the Chinese by barriers of race, language, and religion, Outer Mongolia has traditionally played a rôle of independence which has cast it more than once into the lap of the empire to the north. No alliance ever achieved with Czarist Russia was as strong or as curious as that at present of the People's Revolutionary party of Outer Mongolia with the Communist International. Legally and diplomatically an independent country, the sovereignty of China having been formally recognized by the Soviet Union in a treaty, the country is still ruled by a small party of communists. Most of these are native Mongols who have been trained in Russia. Led by a romantic character named Bodo, these young men seized power in their country in 1921, deposed the Living Buddha, who was the religious leader of the people, and began to modernize their country.

In this task they have had help in men and money and ideas from the Soviet Union. How far this help has become domination, it would be hard to say. The disfranchised priests and nobles have led sporadic revolts which have in the past been put down. There seems to have been, at least since 1925, no large Russian military force quartered on the country. Few observers have had a chance in recent years to examine at first hand the results of the new program. Technical reconstruction of the country, with improved stock-breeding and a few infant industries, has been begun.

The potential importance of the new Outer Mongolia lies not so much in the fact that it is the first territory outside the old Russian Empire to establish a communist government of some permanent strength, as in the technique which is being worked out by Soviet leaders in Moscow and in Siberia in their relations with the Mongols. It is an attempt to conserve local loyalties and traditions within the framework of an entirely new economy, a revolutionary change in the way of life of a whole people. This technique is part of the process which the Russians have had to learn in dealing with component parts of their own country, where Georgians, Armenians, Germans, Jews, and even Mongols are encouraged to develop a nationalism, language, and a cultural tradition within the frame of allegiance to a supernational unit. If it should be successful when applied to people outside the administrative frontiers of the Soviet Union, it would have large meaning for the rest of Asia.

Today the Third International is a quiet office on a side street in Moscow. The theory of socialism in one country, with which Stalin has achieved the leadership of his party, has no such place for external propaganda as is required by Trotsky's theory of permanent revolution. In the whole Soviet Union, as in Siberia, the urgent problem which absorbs more energy, funds, and men than the Bolsheviks can supply is the achievement of a socialist industrial state. Even the efforts to stir up trouble in neighboring countries which were made before 1928 are not likely to be repeated, because of the diversion of national energy to domestic tasks, and the compelling need and desire within the U.S.S.R. for external peace. If recognition by the United States is followed by even a fraction of the trade increase which has been predicted, it is likely to mean a reinforcement of this present Soviet policy.

That this spells the end of what the Japanese call "dangerous thoughts" abroad would be a very hasty conclusion. Industrial machinery in Siberia purchased with American credits may prove to be more dangerous to the established order of things on both sides of the Pacific than Bolshevik agents have ever been. Flood and famine, wars and plagues and great depressions have always led to sedition and civil disturbance in the East as in the West. One of the greatest of the changes brought about by the emergence of Soviet Siberia on the Pacific is that such sedition will have in the future a channel of doctrine and practice which may intensify its danger.

Japan, as already shown, has sought to Westernize itself by importing machines and manufactured goods, and by teaching itself to speak the economic language of the West. Necessarily, therefore, it has sought an outlet for its quickening industrial life in the market closest at hand—the Asiatic continent. Japan presses China in one direction. The Soviets are pressing in another, not at the minute as sellers of surplus goods, but as vital carriers of a new way of living. But the Soviets will not lack effectiveness because they are at present armed with ideas and not with guns, as were the agents of empire in Manchuria.

This is of much greater importance to the countries of the Pacific, and to the nations whose empires of trade and colonies have grown in Asia, than the munitions produced at Magnitogorsk or the machinations of underground conspirators from Moscow. Fifty years before the revolution, Dostoievsky wrote: "Every great people believes and must believe that in them alone is the salvation of the world, that their sole purpose in life is to lead all peoples to the final con-summation appointed for all. The immense arrogance of believing that we can and shall say the final word is the pledge of a nation's most exalted destiny." Even if the theory of socialism in one country has triumphed over the Third International, and even if the present policy of the Soviet Union is based on an imperative demand for peace, the latest eastward thrust of Russia through Siberia is infused with this conviction. It is a far cry from the imperial advance of Czarist Russia. It carries no less freight of meaning, however, and possibly of conflict, for the peoples of the East and for Western empires.

CHANGING MARKETS

CHANGING MARKETS
Grover Clark

IN THE early days of modern trade, Westerners went to the East to buy, not to sell, but at the end of the nineteenth century the West changed its attitude and acted aggressively on the theory that the East is a vast potential market for Western manufactures and a source of raw materials. During and since the World War the Eastern countries, notably, as we have seen, in the case of Japan, have developed their own industries so that now they are well on the way toward supplying their own requirements for the simpler manufactured goods which can be sold in large quantities. Correspondingly, the East is becoming a market for food and cotton and other raw materials and for complicated and high-quality manufactures.

So far, too, Western trade with the East, particularly American trade with China and Japan, has been comparatively unimportant. The West's territorial and other expansion into the East for economic purposes has been in the main a reaching out after hoped-for future opportunities rather than a consolidation of profitable advantages already secured. These future opportunities have remained in good part uncaught will-o'-the-wisps. This striving for economic opportunities has led to considerable conflict in the past; the demand for freedom to trade may breed more conflict in the future, especially if any one country attempts to close the doors of trade to the others.

The "lure of the East" is an old fever in the blood of the West. Alexander was driven by it toward India. The Arabs felt it when they sailed to India and China before the seventh century, and came back with their silks and ivories and their stories of Sindbad and Aladdin. The crusaders had it, along with a sincere religious feeling. Marco Polo took it with him to China, and returned to write a book which spread the infection anew and virulently in Europe. Columbus, Vasco da Gama, Magellan, and the rest of that rough and reckless crew who set out to find sea routes to the East, were drawn by this age-old lure of the East.

Tragedy and loss and death have been the fate of many of those who yielded to the lure. Even in recent decades, of those who have gone to the East hoping for quick wealth, many more have become beachcombers than millionaires. But, through the centuries, a few have profited spectacularly. The tales of failure have been forgotten; those of success have been told, and exaggerated and retold. So the East has continued to attract the West.

The persistence of this "lure of the East" for the

West has been one of the important but often overlooked causes of the West's continuous drive of expansion in the East. Without the will-o'-the-wisp hope of
vast profits, it is quite possible that the West would
have stayed at home.

At any rate, the West has not depended and does
not now depend on the East economically. It could
produce at home, or get along without, the raw materials which, for its convenience or pleasure, it imports
from the East—even the three chief Eastern specialties: tea, silk, and rubber. It could live comfortably
without food or clothing from the East.

Even after these four centuries, too, the West's
economic interests, including direct investments, which
will be dealt with in a subsequent chapter, in the Far
East are comparatively small. The trade figures tell a
similar story. Perhaps, taken as a whole, the West
has made money from its dealings with the East,
though the profits certainly have not been large. If
the costs of wars and of military force for the acquisition or "protection" of interests, and the gifts for
philanthropic purposes, be set off against whatever
business profits there may have been, the balance is
more likely to be in red.

Nevertheless, the West has gone on expanding into the
East for four centuries. During the latter part of the
eighteenth and through the nineteenth century, this
expansion was in part a scramble for territorial and
political aggrandizement rather than simply a search
for new economic opportunities. The theory also was
that a modern nation needed assured access to "undeveloped" regions. Until the latter half of the nine-

teenth century, this access was supposed to be advantageous chiefly because it opened the way to getting goods of various kinds, especially raw materials, which were not produced in the West: goods which could be bought cheaply and sold at a great profit or which would serve as materials for use in industry. Shortly after the industrial revolution was well under way, however, the British discovered that on power looms they could make cotton piece goods—which the West had been importing from the East—cheaply enough to sell at a profit in India and China. So the idea started that the East could be a vast market for Western manufactured goods. That new idea came very much to the fore in the last years of the nineteenth century, and it still exercises a powerful influence on the Western attitude toward the East.

The impulse which sent Columbus and the rest across the Atlantic and around Africa was the desire to buy, or acquire in less commendable ways, rather than to sell. For three centuries and more this continued to be the primary interest of the Western traders in the Far East. They took goods to sell in the East, or on the way there, chiefly to get money with which to buy the tea, silk, chinaware, cotton goods, and other articles of lesser importance which could be sold in the West. The profits on the business were made—or expected—on the imports from the East rather than on the exports to it.

A specific illustration of this situation is supplied by the records of the British East India Company's trade with Canton during the seventeen years, 1793 to 1809, as given by one of the officers of the company.

The costs on goods sent to Canton from England during this period, he says, were £19,069,302, which included nothing for transportation or for payment for the ships' officers, crews, and supercargoes—all these items being charged against the Canton-to-England business. Of this, £13,300,017 (69.8 percent) was for woolen goods, £3,302,321 (17.3 percent) for other goods and stores, and £2,466,964 (12.9 percent) for bullion. On the business in these goods the company lost £956,795. Trading from England to Canton thus was distinctly unprofitable.

Trading the other way was a different matter. The costs on the "exports from Canton to England" amounted to £41,203,422, of which £30,051,881 (72.9 percent) was costs and charges on merchandise, £10,-886,017 (26.4 percent) was freight and demurrage, and £265,524 was customs duties. The receipts from sales in England totaled £57,896,274, which left a "profit on the trade" of £16,692,852 even though the entire expenses of the ships out and back were charged against the return trips. Figuring from the costs as given, therefore, the company lost 5.1 percent on its England-to-Canton trade and made a "profit" of 40.5 percent on its Canton-to-England business.

Modern accounting methods would show a much smaller percentage of profit than this—if they left any profit at all. In the figures as given by this officer there is no record of the capital costs of the ships and warehouses used in doing the business, no allowance for replacement of the capital equipment, though the replacement costs must have been comparatively high since storms and pirates and rival Western traders did so much damage to the company's ships and goods; nor is there any provision for the heavy costs of the armed forces which the company maintained to protect and advance its interests. In spite of these omissions, when the business of the company was discussed, people listened in awe to tales of "profits" of nearly 50 percent. The South Sea Bubble was expanded with the talk of profits which were calculated precisely in this way.

Of the British East India Company's shipments to Canton in these seventeen years, 12.9 percent was bullion. For the years 1785–91 the proportion was 55.0 percent. American traders carried much more than this. One American shipment which sailed from New York for Canton in 1804, for example, took $72,000 worth of bullion and specie in a total cargo of $120,000 —60 percent. A New York merchant said that out of his exports to China in 1824 totaling $1,311,000, nearly $900,000 was in specie—68.7 per cent. In the ten years 1821–30, 73.7 percent of the American exports to China was bullion and specie.

No profit was to be made by trading in this money, as money. The constant shipment of such large quantities of bullion and specie also put a premium on it in the West and caused other difficulties. So the traders sought goods which they could carry on the outward journey, to trade in on the way and to sell in China, to get funds for buying Chinese goods.

This desire for goods to exchange had important consequences. It was one of the principal causes of the start and growth of the practice of taking opium from Turkey and Persia and India into China, which led to so much trouble. The discovery that there was in

China a good market for furs was one of the chief causes of the development of the fur-catching industry on the Pacific coast of the American continent and in the Pacific Ocean, with all the international complications which resulted. The need to sell in order to get funds with which to buy also materially affected what the Westerners did in the East, long before the time came, at the end of the nineteenth century, when the desire for markets rather than for sources of supply became dominant. The East was economically self-sufficient, and it had no particular desire for the goods which the West had to offer. If the Westerners had been content simply to bring out shiploads of silver, to buy what they wanted of Eastern goods, and then to depart, there would have been little or no friction. But the Westerners could not afford thus to pour currency into the East. If they were to buy, they had to sell, whether the East wanted to buy or not. When they found that the selling as well as the buying could be profitable, the traders demanded that their governments support them in opening up new trading centers and protect them in the exercise of "rights" which they had secured by use or threat of force. In this process, a considerable amount of fighting was done.

Armed conflicts began, in fact, very soon after the Westerners first arrived in Eastern waters, and all through the last four centuries armed force has been at the back of Western expansion into the East. The clashes, especially in the early period, frequently were between the agents in the East of the various Western powers, in the course of efforts to secure or keep special advantages or territorial footholds or trade monopolies.

There also were wars with, or more casual military or naval demonstrations against, the Eastern peoples, when these latter objected to what the Westerners were' doing, or when they appeared—to the Westerners —to be insufficiently "respectful" of the treaty rights or other interests which the Westerners had acquired.

That story—the story of the Western imperialistic expansion throughout the world in the eighteenth and nineteenth centuries, and of the incidents of that expansion in the Far East—has been told too often, and the record is too plain on the map and in the collections of treaties, to need retelling here. For our purposes it will suffice to note that Western economic and territorial interests in the Far East expanded steadily but slowly, though they remained relatively very unimportant.

American economic interest in the Far East was fairly active as long as the American population and business were confined largely to the Atlantic coast. At this time, in fact, the trade with China formed a larger proportion of the total American foreign trade than the trade with the entire Far East did at any subsequent period until the World War. When, in the 1830s, the Americans began to turn their attention and energy to the stupendous task of opening up and developing their own vast continent, they lost interest in the Far East even more definitely than they did in foreign trade and ocean shipping generally. After the Civil War, the American government continued to keep in contact with the developments in the Far East, and to insist that Americans there should enjoy trading and other advantages equal to those of any others. American thought, energy, and capital, however, were so completely absorbed at home that little was left over for the Far East. The vast opportunities and staggering demands of the opening of America itself, furthermore, went far toward satisfying all desire for adventure and opportunities for quick wealth.

This first notable change in the trade importance of the Far East to the United States was clearly reflected in the volume of Pacific commerce. Trade with China, which amounted to 6.4 percent of total United States trade between 1823 and 1827, had dropped to 2.1 percent by the years 1848–52, and from 1883 until the World War held fairly steady at about 1.6 percent. With Japan, after Perry had broken its seclusion, United States trade increased slowly. By 1913–17, it constituted 3.5 percent of total American foreign trade. China and Japan together, in the five years preceding American entrance into the World War, accounted for only 5 percent of the foreign commerce of the United States.

Even within these limits, imports have consistently figured more heavily than exports. American goods sold in China made up about 40 percent of our trade with that country in 1823–27; fifteen years later they had dropped to 27.4 percent. They continued at less than 25 percent until the World War, except for the period at the turn of the century, when the young American commercial empire raised its exports to China back to 41.5 percent of its total trade with that country. With Japan the same was true; the years 1898 to 1902, when over 40 percent of the trade was United States exports, constituted the exception in a trade which, except for those years, was preponderantly an import trade. Even when the fabulous markets of the East were most fervently accepted in popular imagination, they failed to absorb as much as the United States imported from them.

The rise of the proportion of British exports to China in its total trade with that country, and the parallel change in American trade with China, which came in the five years at the turn of the century—from 61.9 per cent to 71.6 percent in Britain's case, and from 23.2 percent to 41.5 percent in the case of the United States —are both an indication and a consequence of the sharp increase in Western interest in the East as a market at this time and of the sudden outburst of aggressiveness on the part of the Western powers in securing new footholds and economic advantages in China. China's entire foreign trade reflected this same shift: imports increased 42.8 percent between 1893–97 and 1898–1902, while the exports grew only 32.2 percent.

Several influences operated to cause this comparatively sudden change in the attitude and actions of the Western powers in their dealings with China and with each other in relation to China. One of these was Japan's comparatively quick and easy victory over China in the war of 1894–95—a victory which threw into glaring relief the weakness of China and led the principal European powers to take quick action to prevent Japan from poaching in what they had looked on as their preserve for political and economic exploitation.

Perhaps more important than this, however, was the fact that the Western expansion in regions nearer home, and in the lesser lands of the Far East, which had been proceeding for a century and more, had about reached its limits. Africa had been divided between the European powers. The United States had headed off any further European expansion on the American continents. Russia had pushed its frontiers eastward across Siberia to the Pacific. The Near East had been brought more or less completely under European control, though Turkey and Persia still remained nominally independent. Britain, France, and Holland had taken or preempted India, Burma, Dutch East India, Indo-China, the Malay States, Australia, New Zealand, and most of the rest of the islands and territories along the way from Europe to China or in the Pacific. Japan had saved itself from the fate of the other island territories, first by closing its doors to Western relations, and then by developing, with extraordinary rapidity and skill, its own political, economic, and military organization. By the last years of the nineteenth century, in brief, no place of importance except China remained where the flood of imperialistic expansion from the West could spread.

Japan, stirred by the sight of that flood and seeking a foothold on the continent of Asia as both a military and an economic support, pushed at the gates of the Chinese Empire—the gates which looked so imposing but proved to be so flimsy. The gates collapsed. The Western nations promptly elbowed Japan out of the position which that country had gained in the opening, and began to crowd through themselves.

The story of this period of the "battle of the concessions"—from 1895 to 1900, roughly—like that of events through the nineteenth century, has been told too frequently to need detailed repetition here. There was much talk of dividing China into "spheres of influence," in each of which one of the principal European powers would have economic advantages: Russia in Manchuria; Britain along the northeastern coast of China, in the Yangtze Kiang Valley, and in the southeast; Germany in Shantung Province; France in the north central hinterland and the southwest. Concessions were secured to build railways, for which the foreigners were to furnish all or most of the money, and in which they would exercise varying degrees of control of the operations. These railways tapped the principal centers of population (and hence the principal markets) or gave access to important undeveloped mineral resources, or both. Mining concessions were secured, usually in connection with the railways Altogether, it looked for a time very much as though China in practical fact and perhaps openly and avowedly would be divided into regions each of which would be under the control of one of the principal European powers.

At this same time, the United States fought the Spanish-American War, acquired Hawaii and the Philippines, and definitely emerged both as a positive force in world affairs and as a nation with territorial interests in the Far East. Disturbed by what was happening in the course of the "battle of the concessions" and by the possibility that if the European powers established special "spheres of influence" for themselves, Americans would be crowded out, Secretary of State John Hay reasserted what had been the fundamental principle of American policy in the Far East for a hundred years—the policy to which he attached the term

"Open Door." By this he meant, or seemed to mean, equal rights of every kind for all foreigners doing business in China and, specifically, equal rights for Americans with all others, as is made clear in another chapter.

The sudden increase of foreign expansion in China in the last years of the nineteenth century aroused considerable Chinese antagonism and apprehension, it is true. The shrewd old Empress Dowager and her immediate associates in the Manchu Imperial Court took advantage of this situation to turn against the Westerners the feeling which had been smouldering for fully a century against the Manchus themselves—and breaking out occasionally into flames. The more statesmanlike leaders in government circles and in business, however, saw in the defeat by Japan and the new Western aggressiveness an urgent call to develop in China itself the organizations and institutions which would make possible effective resistance to Western penetration.

From the developments in China in the late 1890s and early 1900s, the Westerners secured a large extension both of their territorial holdings and of their opportunities to reach what they believed was a potentially almost inexhaustible market—a market for surplus capital as well as for manufactured goods. But from these same developments, the Chinese got a strong impetus to modernize their country, and considerable financial and other assistance in furthering the very changes which eventually would make it possible for them to throw off Western political influence and to take control of the economic life of their own country. Railways, modern banks, steamships, and other modern economic agencies which the West introduced in China—and for which the West furnished most of the money at the start—set going in China new economic currents which are proving more profitable, financially, to the Chinese than to the Westerners.

The beginning of the twentieth century saw the Westerners not only stressing markets in their new economic penetration in the Far East, but also turning increasingly from politics to economics in their drive to extend their influence. In the course of the nineteenth century, by political pressure, backed by the use of the threat of force, they had acquired territorial footholds. Where nominal political independence had been left to the Oriental countries—as in China, Japan, and Siam—they had secured substantial political privileges, such as extraterritorial jurisdiction over their own nationals, treaty control of tariffs, and the right to administer the foreign settlements in the principal ports of the several countries. After the twentieth century started, there were no more important seizures by Westerners of Far Eastern territory, and the tide began to turn toward the surrender of the special political privileges.

This turn came in Japan before the end of the nineteenth century, and early in the twentieth the last of the special foreign privileges there were canceled. Early in the 1900s, the United States and Britain intimated in new treaties with China that they would be ready to consider surrendering extraterritoriality and the control of China's tariff if and when China put her house in what the Westerners considered order. Moves for a similar surrender in Siam began not much later. The Americans talked somewhat about independence for the Philippines at some future date.

In brief, the political and territorial advance of the West into the East practically came to an end with the nineteenth century. The cynical might say that this was because the Westerners already had substantially everything they could reasonably or unreasonably want—though to leave it at that would be to neglect the fact that there was in the West a real beginning of the feeling which found expression two decades later in the Wilsonian doctrine of self-determination of nations.

In passing, it is well to notice that when Japan reached a position from which it might have joined in the imperialistic orgy of the Western powers, practically all the possibilities of expansion in the Far East already had been exhausted. When Japan did make the move against China in 1894–95, and secured a foothold on the continent as a result of the victory, the European powers promptly saw to it that it was turned back to its own islands.

The only Western nation which tried seriously to add to its territory in the Far East after 1900 was Russia. It took advantage of the Boxer situation to fill Manchuria with troops, obviously as a preliminary to annexation or a protectorate. The Western powers protested vigorously. Russia yielded and withdrew the troops—but retained control of the railway, mines, and leased territory, the rights to which had been acquired in 1896–98. The political moves in Korea which were leading up to the establishment of Russian control in that country were also continued. Then, in 1904–05, Japan put the final quietus on Russian ambitions in southern Manchuria and Korea by defeating the Russian Empire in war. By that victory over Russia, Japan in effect retook the position in Manchuria which it had taken from China in 1894–95 but had been compelled to surrender. The victory also opened the way to future annexation of Korea and established Japan as the most powerful nation in the Far East and, potentially, as one of the great powers.

Japan's victory over Russia, however, did more than give this continental foothold, this access to the resources of Manchuria, and this new international position. It sent a thrill of pride and self-confidence through all the peoples of the East, from the coasts of China to the Red Sea. For the first time in the history of the contact of the modern West with the East, an Oriental people had conquered in armed conflict a Western nation. The vanquished, moreover, was the largest empire of the West, and the victor a nation which had been thought of throughout the East and West as of little importance. That nation had copied the West's own methods and proved itself superior to the West in their application. What Japan had done, the others could do. Thus the feeling ran. While the seeds of present-day nationalism in the Eastern countries may have been planted before 1900, Japan's victory over Russia was the fertilizer which set those seeds to growing rapidly. That victory also dealt a staggering blow to the prestige of the West in the East because it showed that the Western nations were not invincible.

That prestige was shattered when, beginning in 1914,

the Western nations for four long years fought with each other—and called on the Eastern peoples for help in the struggle. Japan had achieved complete freedom from every kind of formal Western political dominance before the war; the last vestiges of a sense of subordination disappeared when it was given a place among the great powers at the Peace Conference and in the League of Nations. During and after the war, the Chinese began aggressively to demand the ending of special foreign privileges in their country, and to undercut the practical exercise of foreign control whenever and in any way they could: in the administration of the customs and salt services, in the operation of the railways, in the payment of government obligations and the carrying out of concession agreements, in the administration of the missionary schools, in the dealings with individual foreigners and foreign firms. The old acceptance of the foreigner and his claims as sacrosanct disappeared with the World War. In its place came a new desire and determination not so much to oust the foreigner as to deprive him of his privileged position and to subordinate him and his affairs in China to Chinese control.

This change in the attitude of the Chinese had its counterpart in Japan, in the Philippines, in the Malay States, in Indo-China, and elsewhere in the Far East, though the world has heard chiefly of what has been going on in China as a result of the change of attitude. The change there has been most conspicuous because China was in a middle position—neither completely free nor under foreign domination, while Japan, on the one side, was free, and, on the other, Western influence was overwhelming in the lesser East Indian countries.

With the far-reaching political and psychological consequences of the collapse of Western prestige in the Far East and of the up-welling of nationalistic self-assertiveness, however, we are concerned here only in so far as they affected the foreign trading position. The effects were considerable and of several kinds.

When Japan recovered full control of the tariff, for example, it proceeded promptly to apply a protective policy which aided the development of the Japanese cotton-manufacturing industry. This in turn made it possible for Japan to go far toward replacing Britain as the supplier of cotton piece goods to China and the Far East generally. Thus, in this case, Japan's success in shaking off political restrictions which the West had imposed resulted directly in a substantial alteration of the trading position of the West, not in Japan alone, but through the whole Far East. China did not recover tariff autonomy until 1929, and it still is too early to judge what the effects of that recovery will be on the industrialization of the country and on the markets for foreign goods, Japanese as well as Western. Already, however, it is obvious that they are likely to be far reaching and, for a time, at least, to work to the disadvantage more of Japan than of the Western countries.

Already, too, it has become clear that the recovery of tariff autonomy in China is an important factor in the financial relations between China and the other countries—on the market for capital, that is to say. Control of its own tariff has given and will continue to give China substantially more revenue from the customs duties than formerly. China is thus in a much better position than before in bargaining for foreign loans, if they are wanted.

The widespread change of feeling in China—a change not often expressed in so many words but no less real —has been an important factor. It has been a change from the feeling that foreign rights in general should be respected lest neglect bring disastrous consequences to a feeling that obligations to foreigners are to be fulfilled when convenient or if they cannot be avoided. This has had much to do with causing the defaults on the general foreign loans of the government and on many of the private loans.

None of the foreign loans has been formally repudiated. But in the case of the so-called "Nishihara loans" and certain others made by the Japanese, for example, the attitude has been that the claim for repayment is vitiated by the fact that the money was loaned for illegitimate political purposes. In the case of other foreign loans—even loans which were incurred legitimately and for purposes beneficial to China—the sense of obligation to pay has been weakened by the general feeling that China has not been a free agent in her dealings with foreigners and that the obligations to them were assumed under more or less duress.

This point needs to be kept in mind if one is to understand what has happened and is likely to happen to foreign claims on China—claims for the exercise of political rights such as extraterritorial jurisdiction and the administration of foreign settlements, as well as for loan repayments. Commitments made in circumstances in which the Chinese feel that they are acting as fully free agents and in no sense under foreign pressure—as, for example, the American loan agreements for wheat and cotton purchases in the last couple of years—are much more likely to be kept than those accompanied by a feeling of coercion. This feeling, unfortunately, and justifiably or not, exists toward nearly all of the commitments to foreigners except those made very recently.

Furthermore, this newly developed nationalistic feeling of the Chinese, like the similar feeling in other Far Eastern countries, is and will be an increasingly important factor in the development of foreign access to markets there. The time quite definitely has come when the foreign business man seeking to enter the Chinese market must study the country and adapt both his product and his selling methods to the customs and prejudices as well as to the desires of the people. He must act as though China belonged to the Chinese rather than to the foreigner.

The varied expressions of an aroused nationalistic self-consciousness in the East are not the only difficulties which have arisen in the path of Western penetration into Eastern markets. Of a different sort but perhaps more important in this special connection is the extent to which that part of the world has developed the capacity to supply its own need for manufactured goods, especially of the simpler sorts, and to carry on modern business of all kinds without Western aid. There once seemed to be justification for the belief, on which Westerners acted with such sudden vigor at the turn of the century, that the teeming millions of the Far East offer a vast market. (If, for example, each Chinese should spend five cents more a week for American goods than he now does, the increase in purchases in a single year would total more than half the value of all the American exports to China for the last fifty years.) But it is by no means so certain that that market, even for manufactured goods, will remain open to the West. In fact, Western factory products in certain lines, which formerly had virtually a monopoly of sales in the East, have been in large part driven from the field by the competing products of Eastern factories.

The story has been told in another chapter of how Japan imported cotton machinery shortly after the close of the period of seclusion, built up her cotton manufacturing industry and, especially since the World War, succeeded in taking from the British most of the market for cotton goods not only in Japan but also in China and throughout the Far East. More recently, the Chinese have been doing to the Japanese cotton industry what the Japanese did to the British.

Beginning in 1886, the Chinese have built a steadily increasing number of cotton mills in order to supply their own demand for factory-made cotton goods. Starting just before the turn of the century, Japanese, and to a considerably less extent, British, also have built cotton mills in China. A substantial majority of, the cotton mills in China, however, have been and are Chinese owned, though the Japanese and British mills, like the Chinese, are in direct competition with mills in Japan and Britain in supplying the Chinese market.

This modern cotton industry in China now has reached the point where it is able to supply a large part of the demand in that country for the coarser grades of cloth, and even to furnish considerable amounts of manufactured cotton goods for export. China's imports of cotton goods, for example, were taels 182,000,000 in 1913, forming 31.1 percent of her total imports. In 1928 they were taels 190,000,000, but this was only 15.7 percent of the imports. In 1932 the value was down to taels 88,000,000 and the percentage to 8.3. Exports of manufactured cotton goods in 1913 were only taels 2,000,000 and formed only 0.3 percent of the total exports. In 1928 the figures were taels 64,000,000 and 6.4 percent, and in 1931 they were taels 84,000,000 and 9.1 percent. In 1932 the value dropped to taels 53,000,-000, but the percentage climbed to 10.6. A substantial part of the exports consists of cotton yarns shipped to Japan for spinning there into piece goods. But the mills in China, besides having gone far toward closing the Chinese market to foreign manufactured piece goods, also are becoming serious rivals of the mills in Japan in supplying piece goods to the East Indies regions, especially to the large Chinese communities there.

The cotton goods situation presents the most striking illustration of the way in which the development of modern industry in the East is closing the market for the coarser grades of manufactured goods from the West.

The same sort of development is taking place in other lines, though not on so significant a scale as yet. Unquestionably further industrialization will take place. This probably will mean an increase in the purchasing power of the "teeming millions," which at present is very low in per capita terms. That quite possibly will bring a demand for certain kinds of manufactured goods which the West can produce more economically or efficiently than the East is likely to be able to do for a considerable time: high quality goods and complicated or delicate machinery, for example. But the volume of trade in such articles probably will not be great. Already the hope, which not a few in the West had, of being able to make large profits from the sale in the East of large quantities of easily and cheaply made manufactured goods has been destroyed. The people of the East are making and increasingly will make these goods for themselves. In all probability, too, they will follow the Western example of erecting tariff walls as high as may be necessary to make sure that home products have an advantage in the home market.

This does not mean, however, that the West has nothing which it can sell to the East. Surprising as it may seem, the exports of raw materials from the West to the East already have become substantial. Japan, for example, grows practically no cotton, so that the large amounts needed in the cotton industry must be imported. Most of it comes, and is likely to continue to come, from the United States. China also has taken to importing substantial amounts of high quality raw cotton, even though it produces a good deal and exports some of poorer grades. In the past three years, between 8 and 10 percent of China's imports have been raw cotton, principally from the United States.

The East, furthermore, has begun to import considerable amounts of cereals from the West. It is generally understood that Japan's farms do not produce enough to feed the Japanese people, but it will surprise many to be told that China also does not feed itself. Japan's net imports of cereals (total imports less exports) have been falling off recently, in both value and percentage of total imports, while China's have been materially increasing. Thus, in 1913, Japan imported, net, cereals worth yen 61,000,000, or 8.3 percent of her total imports, while the 1932 figures were yen 49,000,000 and 3.4 percent. In 1913 China's net cereal imports were taels 21,000,000, which was 3.6 percent of the total imports; the 1932 figures were taels 189,000,000—nine times as much as in 1913—and 17.8 percent. Rice from Indo-China, Siam, and the neighboring territories formerly made up the bulk of the cereal imports for both Japan and China. In recent years, however, wheat has been shipped in large amounts to the East, chiefly to China, from the United States, Canada, and Australia.

The fact of the matter seems to be that the Far East does not now produce enough food to feed its own people or enough cotton to clothe them. If the trend indicated by the figures for the last two decades continues (and there is no apparent reason for thinking it will not), the East will draw on the West for increasing amounts of the necessities of life—food and material for clothing. The East thus offers to the West a substantial and probably growing market. Contrary to the expectations of many in the West, however, it is a market for products of the farm rather than of the factory.

That being so, the indications are that the Western countries which will benefit from Eastern markets will be those which can produce from their farms substantially in excess of their domestic needs: the United

States, Canada, some of the South American countries, and Russia. The highly industrialized European countries, Britain particularly, which themselves must import food and materials for clothing, apparently will not be in a position to keep or develop a large export trade to the Far East. In the East itself, as China becomes more industrialized and so better able to supply its own demands for manufactured goods and to furnish factory products to its neighbors to the south—and as India approaches industrial self-sufficiency—Japan's position will become even more difficult than it is at present.

Under these conditions, it would appear that of all the nations the United States is best situated to benefit from the Far Eastern market possibilities. Other nations can supply the products of the farms, or the special kinds of factory products, which the East will want from the West. Only the United States can supply the products of both farms and factories, and it can meet on equal terms competition in either kind of product. The United States also probably will be better able than any other Western nation, or than Japan, to supply the capital which the East, particularly China, is likely to want for its development along modern economic lines.

The trade records show that the United States already has begun to benefit from this favorable position. During and just after the World War, American trade with both China and Japan increased steadily and fairly rapidly. The increase was in total value, in percentage of American foreign trade and in the percentages of the foreign trade of China and Japan. The

American trade records show that the United States regularly bought more from China and Japan than it sold to these countries, except that in the five-year period 1928–32 the exports to China were slightly in excess of the imports from that country—although, curiously enough, the Chinese records, owing to a different system of valuing the trade, show a substantial surplus of imports over exports in the trade with the United States during the post-war period.

In spite of these increases, the American trade with these two countries remained a comparatively small part of total American foreign trade—about 10 percent in the years beginning with 1918. This is a very much larger ratio than that of Britain's trade with the two countries to total British trade, however; the British figure is approximately or under 3 percent. Furthermore, the American percentage has increased while that of Britain has declined since the World War.

Another significant aspect of the situation is the marked increase of the share of American trade in total trade of the two Oriental countries—simultaneously with an equally marked falling off of the British share. During and immediately after the war, Japan secured more than a fourth of the total trade of China; after the 1918–22 period, the proportion fell off. In the average for the five years 1928–32, Japan led in the share of China's foreign trade, with the United States a close second. In 1932, however, the United States passed Japan, the percentages being 21 percent and 16.9 percent—though it should be noted that the Chinese customs figures for 1932 give no record for the trade of Manchuria in the last half of the year, and Japan's share of the Manchurian trade was considerably greater than its share of the trade of the rest of China.

The records show that in proportion of foreign trade, the West is very much more important to the East than the East is to the West. Japan especially is dependent on the West for both markets and supplies —since the war, practically 40 percent of its foreign trade has been with the United States. Even more significant than this, perhaps, is the very great degree of Japan's dependence on the United States and China for export markets—roughly two thirds of all of Japan's exports are sent to these two countries. China's total foreign trade is considerably less than that of Japan in value and very much less in per capita terms. Nevertheless, that trade has grown rapidly in recent years and has come to be of substantial importance to the country. To cut off that trade would cause serious economic difficulties in China, but nothing approaching the economic disaster which would come to Japan if its foreign trade were to be stopped. With no country does China do so large a part of its foreign trade as Japan does with the United States; Japan and the United States have the largest shares, but their combined trade with China is only a little larger part of the whole than the trade of the United States alone is of Japan's foreign trade.

As we have seen, the West went to the East, for three centuries and more, to buy rather than to sell. Then, at the end of the nineteenth century and after the tide of Western imperialism had swept across most of the unpreëmpted world, the West reversed its attitude and conceived of the East as a vast potential market, especially for manufactured goods. More recently, however, industrialization in Japan and China has gone so far that to a substantial degree the products of Eastern factories are crowding the simpler kinds of Western manufactured goods out of the Eastern markets. This tendency is likely to continue, so that such markets as there will be in the East will call for machinery and manufacturing materials and goods of high quality. As the standard of living rises in the Eastern countries, this market may grow proportionately.

The industrialization of the East, even in its present only partial development, already has brought a substantial demand on the West for food and cotton. This demand for basic agricultural products, some of which are raw materials for manufacturing, seems likely to grow, even if the demand for simple manufactures falls off. The United States would be in a peculiarly favorable situation to benefit from this possible demand for machinery, high quality manufactured goods, and farm products.

To predict the future of this trade would be hazardous. It has been strangely small, compared with the furor and conflict which the struggle for it has produced. It is changing in character. The tendency toward increasingly intimate trade relations between East and West continues to operate, but the growing determination of the Eastern peoples to keep their markets as well as their territories for themselves is a new and incalculable factor in the situation. The future may see conflicts no less costly than those in the past, but these will be for trade rather than for colonies.

BATTLE OF THE BANKERS

BATTLE OF THE BANKERS
Frederick V. Field

INVESTMENTS, as well as commerce and the contest for markets, have played their part in the course of empire in the East. The operations of the large Western banking houses, especially those of America, make an interesting story. Why have investments been made, and what sort of investments have they been? Do they represent an adventure in profit-making distinct from those of trade and diplomacy, or are they inseparably linked with these other aspects of the external relations of the United States? Have they been successful when judged from the point of view of the direct profits accruing from branch factories or loans, or from that of fostering trade or promoting official foreign policy? Finally, are these investments likely to expand or to contract?

These questions may be partly answered by a brief account of the way American investments in China and Japan have been made, and an examination of their nature and their relation to commerce and diplomacy. But a further step will have to be taken. Really to understand the significance of capital exports to the Far East, it will be necessary to examine the economy which produces capital not used at home. If the production of surplus capital, not absorbed within our own economy, is a permanent characteristic of the United States, then the availability of foreign markets for investment is essential. If it is merely a passing phase, or one subject to control, as wheat or cotton crops may be, then American financial relations in the Far East will be susceptible of careful regulation. The answer to this question is by no means of merely academic importance either to this country, or to those countries which have been importing our surplus capital. If foreign loans represent a consciously chosen policy of the United States, they may be expanded when they are socially useful and contracted when they seem to threaten conflict. If, however, they are an integral part of our economic organization, these investments will continue for good or bad as long as that organization remains intact. And, to follow the latter assumption a little farther, if the effects of these investments are seriously detrimental to our welfare and to that of the people of the East, it would seem that they present a formidable question mark to the continuance of an economy from which they inevitably flow.

At the beginning of 1932 American citizens had invested abroad $15,635 million in Europe, Latin America, Canada, and that area known as "the rest of the world." The aggregate investment to the year 1929, which came to about $1,000 million less than the figure quoted above, has been estimated to have constituted approximately 6.3 percent of the total capital funds at the disposal of American corporations. The growth of these foreign investments had been phenomenally rapid. Go back little more than ten years from 1932, and the aggregate sum is cut in half; at the turn of the first decade of the century it was around $1,500 millions, a figure three times the total American foreign investment for 1900.

In the span of those years another nucleus of capitalist economy had come to maturity: the United States had turned from a debtor to a creditor country. Roughly three quarters of a century behind Great Britain in reaching this stage of economic development, half a century behind France, and decades after Germany, Belgium, and the Netherlands, the United States in the 1920s threatened to replace England as the world's greatest banker. At the outbreak of the World War, English foreign investments were valued at about $20,000 million, French at $8,700 million, German at $6,000 million, with American external investments trailing at $2,500 million. By 1930, though Great Britain still ranked first at its pre-war level, the United States was rapidly overtaking it with a far greater annual gain in net capital exports, which in that year raised the aggregate to approximately $15,000 million.

The rate of increase of American foreign investments from 1913 to 1921 (excluding the government's war loans, as in the case of all these figures) was about $680 million a year; from 1922 to 1930 it was $794 million a year. The National Bureau of Economic Research estimates the rate of increase in foreign investments from

[151]

1922 to 1929 to have been 6.7 percent a year, while American corporate capital funds were increasing at only 4 percent a year.

It is not without reason that the foreign investments with which this chapter is mainly concerned, namely those in the Far East, should so frequently be lumped under that belittling phrase "the rest of the world." For they add up to little. American trans-Pacific investments in 1930, excluding philanthropic investments, expressed in thousands of dollars, were:

British Malaya	27,103
China	196,824
Japan	444,639
Netherlands East Indies	201,333
Philippine Islands	166,245
Australia and New Zealand	419,294
Total trans-Pacific	1,455,438

Of the total foreign investments in 1930, that which had been attracted across the Pacific accounted for only 9 percent, while Latin America had obtained 34 percent, Europe 32 percent, Canada 25 percent. The phenomenon of capital exports, however, is particularly well revealed in China and Japan. In this respect the other trans-Pacific regions share the characteristics of one or the other of these two countries and investment relations with them need not be elaborated. The contrasts between American investments in China and those in Japan merit attention as widely differing examples of a common outward movement of capital from the United States. Similarities between them deserve no less consideration, in order to reveal the nature of the process to which investments in both countries are related. Analysis of the contrasts will emphasize the places of destination of capital exports, China and Japan; analysis of the movement of capital itself will dwell on the sending nation, the United States.

Superimpose upon the figure of American financial investments in China the long history of rivalry over the so-called privilege of lending money to and doing business in that country, and you have a story of futility and defeat. Analyze the figures, and you find that investments have been successfully made in almost inverse proportion to the amount of diplomatic, political, and financial intrigues, both official and private, which have accompanied negotiations. There has been no export of capital whatsoever as a result of some of the most involved and grandiose schemes sponsored by Washington. The point to be made is not that because of official sponsorship or interference certain investments failed or failed to be placed, but that all the fuss was not worth the candle, and that the fuss was predicated upon an economic policy which it is well nigh impossible to carry out.

The $444,639,000 investment in Japan is overwhelmingly in the nature of loans to the Japanese national and municipal governments made to carry out American policy in the Pacific or to alleviate the effects of the great earthquake, and loans to Japanese utility corporations made out of that "surplus" capital which was so abundant in the 1920s. Japan being more than China on a par with the United States in both political and economic development, its financial relations with the

[153]

United States have been more the normal ones between a banker and his client than have those between China and this country. The point of interest to examine in connection with the American-Japanese investment will, therefore, be the rôle of the banker. Why does he want to use his money in that particular way? Where does he get the money which he lends?

China, on the other hand, has exhibited almost all the characteristics of a colonial frontier subjected to the dynamic pressure of the mother country, and in the case of China so many countries claimed filial obedience that, had the child been less mature, nearer at hand, of smaller physical stature, and endowed with a wealthier natural inheritance, what ended in quarrels might have taken wars to settle. The pressure of industrial nations, struggling for markets for export goods and capital, brought Turkey, the sick man of Europe, nearer to colonial status and helped to precipitate the world's greatest war. It was the same pressure being brought to bear on China, the sick man of Asia, that makes up the story of capital investments in the Far East. The Hukuang railways, the consortiums, the elaborate paraphernalia of commercial and diplomatic rivalry in China in the last thirty years, grew on the same forces which built the Berlin to Bagdad Railway: the pressure of goods and capital which cannot be consumed by industrial nations under a profit system. Circumstances peculiar to China or Japan and the rivalry among Western powers for their exploitation have combined to check in Asia the unimpeded export of this surplus which has proceeded elsewhere. This pressure lies at the very root of modern empire in the Pacific. Although it

nearer at hand. There was, further, the fact that at least four nations, Great Britain, France, Germany, and Russia, awakened to the possibilities of imperialist relations with China at about the same time, and for any one of them to oust the others would have been no easy matter. China, too, at the beginning of the nineteenth century, was an uncertain prize.

China was an uncertain prize until it was discovered that it would absorb manufactured goods from the Occident as well as supply teas and silk. The latter, after all, replenished the pockets of the traders only; as a consumer China awakened the interest of European producers. Nevertheless, the factors mentioned above combined to give several European powers, instead of only one, a firm foothold in China and to divert a good portion of the energies of these powers from a direct pursuit of their potential victim to wranglings among themselves.

United States interests arrived on the Chinese scene late; a half dozen other countries had a head start. The only chance Americans had to get a slice of the Chinese pie, or so they thought, was to prevent the others from monopolizing it. Let the citizens of every country, we said, compete on equal terms in the exploitation of China. The Americans were not interested in acquiring territory; they were interested in seeing to it that the acquisition of it or of rights over it by other powers in no way hampered their chances of doing business in such politically earmarked regions. Of almost as great importance as equality of commercial opportunity was the maintenance of the administrative and territorial integrity of the Chinese government. Infringements of this integrity spelled disaster not to moral principles but to chances of pursuing commerce. The policy did not imply so much the protection of the Chinese government as such, as it did the maintenance of an equivalent position among the foreign powers vis-à-vis that government. The integrity of China could be tampered with as long as the tampering was done by the major foreign powers acting in concert (the consortiums), but just as soon as one foreign power got advantages over the others (Japan in Shantung and Manchuria, or Great Britain on the Yangtze Kiang) then equality of commercial opportunity was threatened. Thus the United States was a staunch supporter of the most-favored nation clause in treaties, whereby whatever advantages in China accrued to the citizens of any other foreign power also went to Americans.

At the close of the nineteenth century the position of American merchants in and with China was being seriously threatened by the aggression of other imperialist powers. The territorial partition of China into spheres of influence, if not into colonies, was proceeding with alarming rapidity. The British, too, were finding it excessively difficult to devote the energy required to keep up with the pace of aggression and were searching for a formula which would provide a breathing spell, if not permanent stability, in the relations of foreign powers to China. The Hay Open Door notes of 1898–99 were partly instrumental in changing the form if not in stemming the tide of imperialism.

But the tide bore on, and in a few years Americans in Manchuria found it increasingly difficult to complete contracts or negotiate loans. Following the Russo-

Japanese War of 1905, the Japanese had established a virtual monopoly in southern Manchuria while the Russians remained firmly entrenched in the north. Great Britain, holding a fear of Russian Asiatic expansion in common with Japan, was bound by an alliance to do nothing to hinder the latter's interest in the Far East. France, whose bankers were heavily interested in Russia's Far Eastern investments, supported St. Petersburg. Germany, temporarily squeezed out, was angling for a Sino-American-German Alliance.

In the summer of 1905, Mr. Edward H. Harriman discussed with the Japanese a scheme for financing their newly acquired South Manchuria Railway, but Japan refused and secured the loan from British bankers. Mr. Harriman, then, with the active support of the American consul general in Mukden, sought to finance a railway running parallel to the South Manchuria road, but this endeavor was also frustrated, and the contract went to a British concern. American attempts to purchase outright the South Manchuria Railway and the Russian-owned Chinese Eastern were blocked by the Japanese refusal to sell.

In the meantime Japan, Russia, China, France, and Great Britain had in a series of bilateral treaties agreed to the maintenance of the *status quo*. Even the United States, apparently not recognizing that the *status quo* in Manchuria left little room for its own citizens, committed itself to that policy in the Root-Takahira notes of 1908.

The Taft Administration and "dollar diplomacy" came to power in 1909 and immediately set about the task of breaking the unfavorable spiral of events in the

Far East. With respect to Manchuria, Secretary of State Philander C. Knox launched his famous neutralization scheme. With the object of gaining for Americans a stake in the railways of the region and thereby frustrating Russian and Japanese imperialism, Secretary Knox proposed to Great Britain that the railways of Manchuria be internationalized and, in the event of the failure of this plan, that Great Britain and the United States coöperate in financing and constructing a line traversing the area from north to south. Great Britain received the neutralization proposal with a suggestion that its consideration be postponed; the subsidiary scheme it would not consider unless its ally Japan were included. The State Department then presented the plan to the other powers concerned, only to have it turned down through the influence of Japan and Russia.

The efforts of American bankers and industrialists, consular officials and the State Department availed nothing in Manchuria. After nearly a decade of attempts to secure a footing for American enterprise the door remained closed, Japan and Russia still were able to exercise a veto power over who was to do business, and there was no American investment of importance in Manchuria.

The State Department had, however, not put all its Chinese eggs in one basket. At its instigation a group of bankers already interested in Chinese business—J. P. Morgan & Company, Kuhn, Loeb & Company, the First National Bank, and the National City Bank—in the summer of 1909 became "the American group," prepared to participate in business when business could be secured. For four years these bankers acted as agents of the State Department—willing agents, it is true, because their own interests coincided with the government's.

The government became a full-fledged salesman. The scene shifted from Manchuria to central China; the subject remained railways. The story of the Hukuang railways reaches back to 1898 and involves numerous contracts, agreements, loans, and cancellations, which, though illustrating, perhaps burlesquing, the process of economic penetration, need not concern us here. Suffice it to say that shortly after coming to power the Taft Administration learned that negotiations were under way between British, French, and German bankers, with their respective governments in the not distant background, on the one hand, and China on the other for the financing and construction of vastly important railways in the Yangtze Kiang Valley and south from there to Canton. Documents were taken from the files and dusted to reveal excuses for official Washington objections to the exclusion of American interests. Great Britain objected to this American interference in a scheme which would otherwise shortly be consummated. The United States was adamant, and bankers of the four powers foreign to China began negotiating a system for dividing the spoils. The American State Department hoped to see these pourparlers result in the formation of an international banking consortium which, through the strength of its members, would be in a position to control foreign enterprise in China and, by holding each other in check, open wide again the door of equal commercial opportunity.

[161]

German, French, and British bankers put up such obstacles to American participation that President Taft resorted to the extraordinary procedure of personally cabling the Regent of the Chinese Empire. Adjustments had to be made, and they were made, but the quarrels in making them took exactly ten months. And then, all that had been settled was the matter of how the financing and construction were to be divided among the four countries. China had not yet been persuaded to accept the scheme. In the spring of 1910 governments of the United States, Great Britain, France, and Germany urged upon China an early conclusion of the transaction. Another year of wrangling, and China signed the loan agreement which also provided for construction of the railway. A year later the loan was issued in London, Paris, Berlin, and New York, the American share coming to $7,299,000. On the section allocated to American interests, conditions in China have been such that no construction whatsoever has been carried out.

What was accomplished? A relatively small investment was negotiated for a supposedly productive enterprise. The centralization of railway administration in China and the consequent lessening of provincial autonomy, a by-product of the negotiations, was a contributing cause of the 1911 revolution. The imperialist process was subjected to some form of control by the formation of a powerful international consortium of bankers. Americans once more had a position vis-à-vis China equivalent to that of three of their principal rivals. The door was being pried open.

The American group in the Consortium continued

throughout the Taft Administration to be the principal agent through which the government's Far Eastern policy was carried out. Japan and Russia demanded and obtained for their bankers participation in the combination. Neither country being an exporter of capital, the reasons for their interest in the Consortium were obviously political. The intrusion of political considerations into an organization intended to function primarily as a commercial unit destroyed it as an effective instrument of the Open Door policy. During the latter months of Taft's tenure of office, the Consortium's negotiations became involved in disputes with China over provisions for controlling the expenditure of a pending loan, disputes among the six Consortium governments over the personnel for supervising and administering the loan, difficulties over the issue price and exact purposes of the loan, and troublesome competition from banking interests outside the Consortium. European and worldwide political affiliations and objectives governed the transactions. Such were the dissensions that certain of the groups threatened independent action. Even the scope of the Consortium's activities was restricted to administrative loans, thereby excluding industrial and railway loans. Clearly, the Consortium was no longer serving American Open Door desires; on the contrary, it had become the channel for all sorts of demands for special privileges and for greater foreign interference in the domestic affairs of China than ever before.

In consequence, one of President Wilson's first acts upon assuming office in 1913 was to withdraw the government's support from the current negotiations. The American group, as agents of the government, immediately followed suit. The World War followed, eliminating the export of capital from Europe, and the Consortium, for all practical purposes, became non-existent.

Imperialist competition for investments and trade in and with China, nevertheless, persisted. The temporary elimination of European powers and the hiatus in American attention to the Far Eastern situation left the field wide open for Japan. Despite its position as a capital-importing country, Japan managed between 1916 and 1919 to export to China in the form of loans alone almost $100 million. The greater part of these loans were frankly political, but Japanese investments in business enterprises in Shanghai and in Manchurian railways likewise showed enormous increases. In 1914, for instance, Japan owned approximately 12 percent of the cotton spindles in China; by 1919 it owned 22 percent. Likewise Japan's share of the total foreign trade of China in 1914 was 20.7 percent and in 1919, 34.6 percent. The loan transactions, particularly, involved serious infringements on China's administrative integrity, and Japan's assumption of German spheres of influence infringed upon China's territorial sovereignty.

The commercial door was again closing to American business men. The Wilson Administration, therefore, in 1918 launched a proposal for a new consortium. The syndicate of bankers was to have decided advantages over the former one: it was to cover all sorts of loans, industrial, railway, and administrative; its members were to pool all their special rights, and none was in the future to act independently without the consent of the others; it was to include all banking groups having interests in China; it was to stress the economic up-building of China, a process which would provide benefits to the business men of all foreign countries.

Problems in the imperialist struggle for investments arose during the two years which it took to form the new Consortium. The first concerned the degree of government support to be accorded the national groups of private bankers. The United States wanted governments to grant exclusive support to the consortium groups, thereby eliminating the feasibility of independent financing of Chinese enterprise. The British government, however, was unable to form a large enough group of bankers to feel justified in giving it exclusive support. The leading British bankers in Chinese affairs refused to enlarge the group because, to the extent they did so, the share of profits accruing to each member decreased. Great Britain, therefore, informed the United States that, having failed to form a group upon which they could confer a monopoly of official support, they proposed accepting the present smaller group to which they would accord "the fullest measure of support possible." The French government took a somewhat similar position in view of the exclusion of important banks from the French group. The United States had to compromise on this point and thus forsake certain of the open door guarantees implicit in a complete financial monopoly.

The second problem was a vital threat to the Open Door policy. Japan strongly objected to pooling its special rights and interests with an international syndicate, and suggested that "all rights and options held by

Japan in the regions of Manchuria and Mongolia, where Japan has special interests, should be excluded from the arrangement for pooling." In other words, as far as Manchuria and Mongolia were concerned, the privilege of doing business should not be equally open to all, Needless to say, the Japanese formula was not accept- able to Americans, British, or French. A full year was spent attempting to find a compromise solution. During that period a representative of the American group journeyed to Japan in order to explain the American position. The understanding finally arrived at pledged the other foreign powers to undertake nothing inimical to the vital interests of Japan in China and specifically excluded from the scope of the new Consortium a large number of Japanese-owned or -controlled railways or railway projects and subsidiary enterprises, such as mining, in Manchuria.

Ironically, the new Consortium, officially formed in the fall of 1920, has done no business. Although exerting a negative influence valuable to the American policy by halting the scramble for loans, the state of the market for Chinese securities, together with vociferous Chinese objections to this new weapon of foreign im- perialism, has blocked whatever constructive policies the new Consortium might have carried out. Expenses incurred by American bankers incident to participation in the old and the new Consortiums by the end of 1932 reached nearly $900,000. Thomas W. Lamont estimates that the net loss to date from the American group's share in the Consortium's financial operations comes to almost $4,000,000.

Conspicuous though the events just related have been

in American Far Eastern policy, they have not netted much in the way of investments. The loans to China held by Americans in 1930 came to a little over forty million dollars, of which the old Consortium group had been responsible for about one fifth. The bulk of the rather meager American investment in China is not in loans, but in business investments, in the form of automobile agencies, shipping companies, public utilities, banking, real estate, and, most important of all, import and export enterprises.

The nature and methods of doing business in China have already been suggested and need not be elaborated in an exposition of the direct investments. The American policy of providing its citizens with opportunities equivalent to those held by the most favored other foreign powers in China bore directly on the business man. The privilege of doing business under the system of extraterritoriality belongs to Americans as well as British or Japanese. Americans share in whatever advantages accrue to foreign enterprise in China from treaty ports, concessions, and settlements. American citizens actually share in the foreign government of Shanghai, the largest and most important commercial metropolis in China. American corporations in China have the further advantage of federal incorporation in the United States, as well as certain tax exemptions in the United States.

In short, commercial relations between the United States and China, as between other imperialist powers and China, were those characterizing mother country and colony. In the case of many colonies it is pertinent

[167]

to ask whether a balance sheet of assets and debits would not show the final figure in red. With respect to China, where so much of the energy of the foreign powers was diverted from the economic welfare or development of the "colony" to struggling among themselves, it is extremely doubtful if the balance sheet of any one of those powers would reveal profits. For individual interests, such as the Standard Oil Company or the British-American Tobacco Company, the balance sheet probably shows a profit, but it does not follow that the general balance sheet for American enterprise in China does likewise. On the credit side put a yield on a $200 million investment at from 6 to 7 percent a year—and you would be generous in doing so—and add to this whatever profits accrued to those engaged in trade; in the debit column allocate a fair portion of naval expenses, the cost of maintaining marines in China, the cost of consular and diplomatic offices, chambers of commerce, a goodly portion of the Far Eastern Division of the State Department, certain shipping subsidies, the cost of administering the American end of the Consortium—add the two columns, and what have you?

In contrast to the dominant position of business investments in China, the American investment in Japan is composed largely of loans. The Department of Commerce has estimated that at the end of 1930 the direct business investment amounted to approximately $61,-450,000, while outstanding loans to the Japanese government, municipalities, and corporations came to $383,189,000. It is not believed that the business investment has increased by any significant amount since 1930. An additional loan, however, was floated in New York in 1931, which, added to a revised estimate of loans outstanding as of the end of March, 1933, brings the figure for the outstanding portfolio investments to $410,404,480.

A point of particular significance is the degree to which the balance of loans outstanding has been repatriated. The New York Agency of the Yokohoma Specie Bank estimates that more than 80 percent of all Japanese external bonds are at present owned by Japanese citizens. Applied to the balance of $410,404,-480 originally issued in the American market, this estimate implies that approximately $328,327,584 is now owned in Japan.

The way in which the investment in Japan has been placed, moreover, differs radically from the case in China. Although there has been some association of bankers with government policy, the connection has been nothing like that of the China Consortiums. With Japan, American bankers have acted almost entirely in their capacity as bankers, and not as agents of the State Department. Relations with borrowers in Japan, furthermore, have been those usual to solvent clients. There have not been problems of the control and administration of loan expenditures, nor has any problem arisen among the bankers of various countries for the privilege of lending money to Japanese. It cannot be said that any special persuasion has been exerted to "force" Japanese to borrow.

The export of capital from the United States to Japan nevertheless must interest us because, although lacking the political characteristics of expansionism or imperialism, it exhibits certain of its economic characteristics. It is an example of capital export to a country buying less in the United States than it sells. Providing Japan with capital, therefore, cannot be directly associated with the financing of a balance of exports in American trade. Though indirectly it may do so through the use of dollars exported to Japan by other foreign countries in purchasing American goods, it would strain credulity to believe that this furnished a motive to those distributing Japanese bonds in this country. These loans would therefore seem to be associated with whatever in Japan attracted American dollars, or with whatever in the United States impelled them beyond its borders, or with elements of both.

Let us for the moment turn our attention to certain financial aspects of the loans which may reveal the substance of the attraction of capital. Data are unfortunately not at hand whereby these loans to Japan may be compared with domestic issues of the same date, but it may be safely suggested that few domestic bonds offered the same degree of profit or security.

Twenty-two Japanese bond issues have been floated and purchased in the United States since 1905 aggregating $682,820,000. Of this amount approximately $147 million was issued before the World War and the remainder since 1923. Principally from evidence given at the Senate investigation of foreign loans held in the winter of 1931–32, it is possible to present details on $545,320,000 of the American loans to Japan, that is on all issues except three floated in 1905 in connection with the Russo-Japanese War. On these nineteen issues:

American bankers paid Japanese borrowers—	$478,688,400
American purchasers of the bonds paid the American bankers and brokers managing and distributing the bonds—	$503,568,000
Japan has paid or will pay bond owners at maturity of bonds in addition to annual interest charges of from 5 to 7 percent—	$545,320,000

Or, to present the same data differently:

On 19 issues having a face value of—	$545,320,000
The American bankers and brokers took a discount of—	$24,878,700 or an average of 4.56 percent
The purchasers of the bonds took a further discount of—	$41,752,900 or an average of 7.65 percent
Leaving for actual export to the Japanese borrowers—	$478,688,400 or 87.78 per cent of the face value

In viewing the American financing of Japanese enterprise in historical perspective, the conclusion is inescapable that, in their search for profit, American bankers and investors are financing Japanese into a position where they can compete with them in imperialist terms. It is interesting to note that a large proportion of these loans have been made to Japanese electric concerns and that during the last twelve months American manufacturers of electrical equipment have repeatedly charged their Japanese rivals with dumping similar equipment on the American market. At one time Great Britain was in a relation to the United States and Germany analogous to the American position vis-à-vis Japan around 1900. By vast exports of capital to industries in the United States and Germany, Great Britain aided in the development of nations which subsequently became rivals to British external enterprise. Similarly, it appears that with the encouragement of foreign capital Japanese business will more and more severely challenge the industrial position of the countries which have loaned it money.

Consideration of American loans to and investments in China and Japan reveals conspicuous differences with respect to our relations with those two countries. The manner in which loans, for instance, have been negotiated, the nature of the loan contracts, and the purpose for which the capital was loaned are quite different with respect to China and Japan. So important do these differences appear to be that the question arises whether the export of capital to one of the countries is an aspect of the same process operating in the case of capital exports to the other. Is there a common force at work which simply manifests itself in ways superficially unlike each other, or are investments in China and Japan unrelated?

A characteristic of most dissertations on imperialism is either that, in defining the process too narrowly, they leave out of account important and seemingly allied questions which demand analysis, or else that, in attempting to explain everything, they explain nothing.

The concept, imperialism, is ill defined; it is regarded by some to represent the territorial expansion of industrialized countries in the eighteenth and nineteenth centuries; by others as atavistic expansion tendencies, decreasing in vigor, of modern societies; and by still others as embracing the whole range of operations in a highly developed stage of capitalism. In consequence of such disagreement, and in consequence of the widely prevalent use of the concept by liberal, socialist, and communist groups, the term among conservatives has fallen into disrepute. Repeated use of the word, imperialism, in this chapter, therefore, requires explanation.

It is believed that the word, though antagonistic to many persons, expresses better than any other those external relations of a nation which can be attributed to the operations of a capitalist system of economy. Theoretically, it is possible to imagine what the relations among different areas of the world would be if social welfare were the dominant criterion rather than commercial gain. The production and distribution of goods and services would presumably be geared to the equitable welfare of all concerned, to which considerations of commercial profits and losses would be subordinated. The exchange of goods, capital and people among the different areas of the world would be premised on broad considerations of the welfare of the receiving as well as of the sending or selling groups. The agencies in the process of production and distribution, such as shipping and railway lines, banks and other credit organizations, would operate as mere agents rather than as entrepreneurs seeking gain and in so doing possibly jeopardizing large public objectives. Vague as thoughts on such an organization of society may be, they are sufficiently definite to indicate certain contrasts with the existing form of capitalist economy and therefore to make it possible to isolate aspects of foreign relations peculiar to that economy. It is these aspects which the word imperialist is here used to describe.

Implicit in the use of the term is the suggestion that imperialism is an undesirable process and that it springs from a capitalist system of economy. Most of the studies devoted to expansionism support such a contention. They deplore the effects of imperialism and attribute its origin to the industrial character of the expanding nucleus. They differ as to whether doing away with imperialism simply means a reform of the capitalist system from which it springs or a destruction of it. Is imperialism a characteristic of capitalism which can be dispensed with or is it part and parcel of capitalism?

Modern capitalism depends for its continuance and development upon the accumulation of profits. Continuance of an industry involves the constant replenishment of capital equipment in the form of new machines and technical devices whereby production costs may be kept down and competition with other producing units maintained. Development of an industry which is increasing its scale of production requires further new equipment. In both cases a constant stream of fresh capital is required. This capital may come either from the accumulated profits of the industry itself, put by in the form of reserves, or from the public through stock and bond issues. In the latter case, the public will subscribe to the issue only if the industry concerned promises future profits, in the former the industry's reserves come directly from profits. Profits, then, lie at the core of the whole system.

There are two principal ways in which profits may be increased, and both, of course, involve widening the margin between costs of production and total income. Producing and selling more goods up to the capacity of the particular plant decreases the cost of producing each unit by distributing costs over a larger number of units. The amount of goods produced is determined by the prospect of profits, which in turn regulates the flow of capital into new industrial equipment. Closely associated with this method of reducing the unit cost of production is that of decreasing the money cost of labor by expanding the profit item at the expense of wages. The income of industry is divided into rent, interest, wages, and profits. Rent and interest are usually fixed charges; wages and profits are flexible. In view of the importance of profits in order that new capital may be attracted, there is a natural tendency to expand them, to lessen the share of income turned over to wages, and therefore to decrease the purchasing power of the workers. The effect of increased efficiency may be similar. The employment of fewer workers through technical improvements and the lessening of wages of a larger number of workers both decrease the ability of the masses to buy back the goods which they produce.

Capitalist economy thus presents two contradictory trends: the one towards an ever increasing production of goods, the other towards a decrease, or at least a slower increase, in the power of workers to consume these goods. The result is that a market for "surplus" goods, goods which cannot be sold in the domestic market on account of a deficiency in the distribution of purchasing power, must be found abroad. At one stage in history Great Britain possessed a seemingly unlimited market for its surplus manufactures in the markets of Europe and in colonial regions. Gradually, European nations began also to produce industrial goods in excess of the consuming possibilities of their home markets and joined Great Britain in the feverish search for external markets. As soon as these foreign markets became competitive, and it was at this stage that the United States joined the procession, each nucleus began to develop its own special markets and protect them from its competitors—that is, all except Great Britain, which, having a huge head start, did not have to resort to the new system as completely as did other nations until after the World War.

Consequent upon the expansion of production came an increased demand for the raw materials which go into the industrial process and for security of access to the sources of those materials. And thus, in addition to the forcing of foreign markets, a second aspect, protection or acquisition of the sources of raw supplies, was added to imperialism.

China played a peripheral part in this process. It has been pointed out earlier that for various reasons China never came under the exclusive exploitation of any one foreign power, but remained a territory to be quarreled over by a half dozen. In the competition to secure special rights and privileges for the disposal of surplus manufactures or for the possession of raw materials in China, investments have played a conspicuous rôle. As has been emphasized in the case of the United States, these investments were significant not so much in the export of financial capital as in the utilization of investment agencies to alleviate the problem of surplus production.

That these agencies were used at all suggests the enormous strides made by financial institutions in the economy of the industrialized nations. Fifty years ago markets were not sought through the agency of banks, nor did the export of capital through loans assume the importance that it does today. Capital export, indeed, is chronologically the third main characteristic of imperialism and is widely regarded as having become in the twentieth century the most conspicuous attribute of that process. In the case of China it has been suggested that capital exports were not of themselves important; their significance lay rather in their connection with diplomatic policies which were in turn chiefly predicated upon the promotion of trade. Capital exports to Japan, on the other hand, seem to have been carried out as a phenomenon more or less isolated from the development of foreign markets for goods or foreign sources of raw materials.

We have seen that Japan has been able to attract capital from the United States by offering a high degree of security, a high yield on bonds, and a generous discount to bankers and purchasers. These factors, however, would have no power of attraction did they not compare favorably with other investment opportunities, and particularly those in the United States, at the same time. In addition, therefore, to whatever attracted capital away from the United States, there must have been domestic forces operating to expel capital from this country.

It has already been suggested that the keynote of capitalist industry is, of necessity, the accumulation of profits. Largely out of these profits and attracted by them comes the new capital necessary to replenish and expand industrial equipment. The distribution of these profits is unequal, the larger portion going to a relatively small class of the community. All of the income of this wealthy minority cannot be spent purchasing the goods produced by industry; there is an obvious limit to the consumption of goods by any individual. A considerable part of this income therefore flows back into investments which are used to expand industrial equipment. Although industry for a long time was able to use its expanding equipment fully and profitably, the time was reached when even recourse to "forced" foreign markets did not dispose of all the goods that could be turned out. Industrial profits, therefore, and particularly the anticipation of future profits, could not command new capital as easily as formerly. A production plant equipped to produce more goods than it could profitably sell could not offer new capital the same allurements as one operating at full capacity and with prospects of successful expansion. But still the profits accumulated in the past and now concentrated in a few hands sought investment, and just as surplus manufactured goods had been sold externally, so the holders of capital sought foreign markets for investment. When to this was added the high profits offered by industrially ambitious nations like Japan, the export of capital proceeded.

Once started, there is a strong likelihood that the process of lending money abroad will continue simply in order to save the investments already made and regardless of the original forces of attraction and expulsion, even though these are likely to continue. And so with respect to Japan mere refunding operations will probably maintain for some time the outstanding balance of American loans in that country.

The following questions arise from the preceding discussion: Are the trends in economic systems increasing or decreasing the creation of such surpluses? Can capitalism find a cure within itself for chronic underconsumption, or does the cure imply the destruction of capitalism? Without entering into a full consideration of these questions certain comments may be hazarded.

Whether in continental United States, the British Commonwealth, the Japanese Empire-Manchoukuo combination, or Soviet Russia, the modern trend is clearly towards as self-contained an economy as possible. By reductions in industrial and agricultural production, by reëmployment and higher wages, by a wider distribution of the national income, the various capitalist nations or groups of nations are attempting to balance production and consumption. Two principal alternatives for maintaining the domestic balance against external forces are at hand: either the domestic market may be protected against foreign competition by tariffs, or else the important commodities of the world may be controlled by international action. In either case the trend points to the creation of smaller "surpluses" of goods and capital, to a greater ability of the domestic market to absorb the products of industry, and to a somewhat more equitable distribution of income.

In view of the growing number of competing centers of industrialization in the world, it is extremely doubtful if the alleviation of outward pressure in several represents a net gain. While the urge to force external markets or secure foreign supplies on the part of the United States and other powers may somewhat lessen, an increasing number of countries continue to produce surpluses. A case in point in regard to manufactured goods is Japan, and at its present tempo of development it is logical to expect its pressure of goods and even of capital on the rest of the world to increase rather than to diminish.

There is, moreover, little indication that a balance between domestic production and consumption can actually be established within the framework of capitalism. Such a balance implies the control of the quantities of goods produced, and such complete direction of the distribution of savings that the result would have no affinity to an economy based on profits.

Short of radical changes in our economic and social systems, which have little chance, perhaps, of taking place in the near future, the process of imperialism in the Pacific is likely to continue. And with what consequences, it is discouraging to contemplate. As long as the United States continues to produce more goods and to save more capital than it can use at home, it will be interested in the China market. As long as other Western nations, and now Japan, continue to do the same, the struggle between them to lend money to the bankers of Shanghai is likely to persist. As long as the creation of surpluses is directly geared to private profit in the industrial nations of the world, the undeveloped regions of the Pacific face only two alternatives. They must undertake the desperate task of capital accumulation themselves, starving the present to finance their future needs. If they should choose this method, they would look not across the Pacific but to the north, to the Soviet Union, for their only model. The other alternative is to borrow in the money markets of the world, to play the game and run the dangers of modern empire.

SECOND EL DORADO

SECOND EL DORADO
H. Foster Bain

CONFLICT became inevitable as contacts between the West and the East multiplied. Two markedly different cultures were brought into juxtaposition and, as regards stages of industrial development, it was much as if we of the West had been brought into contemporary competition with our own ancestors. Not that our forefathers had not worked out a mode of life admirable in itself and possibly superior in particulars to our own, but in the years since they lived we have developed other methods, other means, and other ideals. If one looks for the essential difference, it will be found in large part in the modern Western emphasis on the value and availability of things. We use a whole range of materials that were but inert stones to our fathers, and we apply widely in everyday life a variety of forces which were unknown or unappreciated by them.

Undoubtedly the greatest difference between modern life in the West and that of earlier years, or that of

[185]

more recent years in the Far East, is found in this emphasis by ourselves on material wealth. Of this, mineral wealth is at once the most enduring and that least used in previous centuries. The application of steam, and later of electricity, has remade the day-by-day life of the peoples of the West, and steam and electricity depend upon metals and in major development on mineral fuels. When peoples armed with such forces and materials encountered great regions where neither had gone beyond the most minor development, it was not unnatural that a great field for further development appeared like a rainbow of promise in their sky. Nor was it unnatural that the Westerners, sure of their knowledge, entered on a race among themselves to possess or to control the key situations in this development.

In keeping with the methods of the time, the first effort was by actual conquest. Later this changed degree by degree into attempts to secure financial control and management. Appreciation of the value of minerals became conscious so much later than that of the value of the famed spices and specialties of the Far East, the purchase of which, as has been pointed out in the chapter on trade, furnished the original stimulus for Western trade with the Pacific countries, that the contest for mines has been in major part not by arms but by negotiation, purchase, and loans. Japan, the late-comer to the game, has recently reverted to earlier methods and marched armies to the centers of control of mineral regions.

Assuming that in fact as in widespread belief great mineral deposits awaited exploitation, such attempt to control them was inevitable in the period before the resident peoples learned modern technique and accumulated capital sufficient to undertake the development themselves. The modern world sees no reason why it should starve for an essential material such as rubber or tin because the natives of the country in which these occur prefer to devote themselves to hunting and fishing. The modern adventurer in business and in industry recognizes no reason why devotion to philosophic ideals other than his own should inhibit development of known resources in any country. He sincerely believes, it is true, that this will be of benefit to the people of this country as well as to the world, but his immediate motive is profit, and his underlying urge is that of all men: to function in the field that he knows best. And so the rush of Westerners into the East as into a vacuum was inevitable. It remains to review the situation and determine whether the search for mines has been any more profitable than have the struggles to secure markets for trade and investments, and what would have been or would be the effect on the world of a slower progress under native guidance.

Lives of peoples have been in all times conditioned by their environment whatever their race heritage may be. What one has to do with is equally important with what one wills to do. When men lived by hunting and fishing only, the fertility or lack of fertility of the soil was of but little moment and the presence or absence of minerals rarely of any at all. When they advanced to grain culture, fertility and water supply became of first importance; the presence or absence of mineral wealth still concerned them but little. It was only when men acquired such knowledge of and control over the forces of nature as to use mechanical power in large amounts, and particularly when through the discovery and application of electricity it became possible to transport and deliver power wherever it was wanted, that minerals became of first importance among the elements in human environment.

Progressive advances in the knowledge of the materials which surround us and of the ways of utilizing them, have profoundly influenced the whole fabric of our lives. Our hunting and fishing ancestors suffered no conscious deprivation from the absence of coal in their neighborhood, and a national strike of the miners, should such a thing have been possible, would have inconvenienced them not at all. Now a large and steady supply of mineral fuel is fundamental to the life and power of any nation that aspires to front or even to middle rank in importance. The substitution of water power for slave labor in grinding the corn of ancient Italy threw thousands of slaves out of work and produced social and political consequences of first rank. How much more does interruption of fuel supply upset the peace and progress of a modern nation when so large a part of the now necessary work of the world is done as a result of burning fuel? Indeed, the strength of modern nations, both in peace and in war, is no longer a function of their population alone but of that plus, or times, the mechanical power per capita used. Many interesting calculations have been made of the effective power of various nations by combining the two sets of figures to measure the work output of nations, for it is what is actually accomplished that counts.

SECOND EL DORADO

Dr. Thomas T. Read, Professor of Mining in Columbia University, has made careful studies which lead to such conclusions as that China, with four times the population of the United States, does about one seventh as much work. British India, with about six times the population of France, exerts but a minor fraction more force; Japan, with a population roughly approximating that of Germany, uses about one seventh the energy. Clearly the possession of those minerals which in use operate like magic to increase the strength and power of each unit of population is of vital importance under modern conditions of competition.

Among the minerals the fuels stand out as of first importance, since they are the main sources of the energy which supplements that of man himself. Water power, while important in specific localities, makes by no means the major contribution. In the United States, which is one of the countries best endowed with potential water power, it is estimated that if all the available sites known were developed, the total power would amount to only about one fourteenth of our present installed capacity. Water power, too, is fixed as to location and only its product can be moved from place to place. Coal, gas, and oil are readily transported, and the capital cost of installation of a steam-electric plant is almost invariably much less than that of a hydroelectric. Not for nothing has coal been called "the mainspring of civilization." It was coal that made possible most of our modern tools, comforts, and luxuries and so created civilization as we now have it. With coal are allied petroleum and natural gas, high quality fuels, each having peculiar characteristics which give

[189]

them preference in use in many fields, but each much more sparingly distributed in nature than coal. Possession of adequate fuel resources within a country or assurance of an uninterrupted supply from without its borders, is essential to any nation which attempts to play a major rôle in this modern world. Truly a nation without fuel is under bonds to keep the peace.

Not fuel alone, but metals are also necessities in these times of intense industrialization. Without steel it would be impossible either to generate or use steam in quantity, and without copper it would not have been possible to build up the immense electrical industry of the present or to send power widespread over the country into each locality that needs it. Without sulphur our modern chemical industries would be impossible, and to them also sodium is almost as important. Other metals and minerals play their part in this modern work, and each in its own field is important if not essential. It is unnecessary to review them all, and it is sufficient for present purposes to point out that for an industrial nation of today a liberal supply of minerals is as essential as pasturage was to the Mongols or the Nile flood to ancient Egypt. With this in mind, it is possible to forecast the future of a nation by reviewing what may be known as to the mineral resources at its disposal. Contests to possess specific territories have frequently been motivated by the desire to control the mineral resources existing or supposed to exist in such territory, and inaccurate data have been responsible for many unfortunate policies by various peoples.

One of the fertile sources of trouble in China, both

between the people of that country and foreigners, and at times between various foreign groups themselves, has been the contest to acquire control of its supposed great mineral resources. That China abounds in such wealth is one of the long-lived traditions. Among Europeans it goes back to the tales of Marco Polo, who traveled in that country in the thirteenth century. As contrasted with medieval Europe, China was then truly rich and powerful, and it is not surprising that the stories the Venetian brought back of the gold and silver table services and other evidences of wealth in Cathay imparted a golden glow to the whole country, a glow that persisted until very recent years. To this tradition the great German traveler and geologist, Baron Ferdinand von Richthofen, contributed mightily by his account of the large numbers of ironworks he saw in Shansi in particular. To all this, a further circumstance contributed which in America at least was a power in shaping public opinion. Few travelers penetrated the interior and of those few almost none had any familiarity with minerals. Missionaries, who saw most of the interior, and who for a time, at least, among foreigners knew the country best, were naturally unskilled in either mineralogy or geology. They were concerned with other things, and entirely unfamiliar with the importance of the quantitative factor in the development of a mineral industry. They had the confidence of the people around them, and to them were brought many specimens of curious rocks, such as have always interested Chinese, and of minerals many of which the Chinese knew well. The account of these things went home in family letters, and so American opinion was shaped to the belief, correct in itself, in the widespread occurrence of minerals throughout much of China.

Unfortunately quantity, as well as presence of quality, is essential to the opening of mines, building and operation of smelters, and, in short, to the establishment of a mineral industry. An occurrence of ore or of coal, quite ample to support a Chinese native ironworks where the annual output is but a minor fraction of one day's product of a modern furnace, is of no importance whatever in this modern world. It was just this fact that was not appreciated until accurate studies of the mineral resources of China came to be made by trained foreign engineers and the National Geological Survey. It is now known that with certain notable exceptions China is poor rather than rich in minerals and if it becomes industrialized it must become on balance an importer rather than an exporter of minerals. The evidence on this point has been recently reviewed and is abundant and conclusive. It rests not on the observations of one man or group but upon those of many, and is the result not of one year's work but the cumulative return on nearly two decades of study by many competent men. Such work is never complete, and new discoveries may reasonably be expected to be made for many years to come. Unfortunately, additional information has so far tended to reduce the estimated reserves rather than to increase them.

Coal and iron are bulky, and transportation adds markedly to their cost. Their occurrence in adequate quantity, of the necessary qualities, and in reasonable juxtaposition is essential to development of steel-making, itself in turn essential to any large-scale manufacture of the tools and appliances of modern industry. To make a ton of pig iron, later to be converted into steel by the use of more fuel for heat and power, there are required approximately two tons of ore, a ton or a trifle less of coke, itself made from one and a half to one and two thirds tons of coal, and, finally, a half ton of limestone and four or five tons of air. The last is, fortunately, everywhere abundant, and finding the necessary limestone for flux rarely imposes great hardship or greatly influences the cost of the product. The ore and the coal, however, involve greater difficulties. Not all iron ore is suitable and the iron content as well as the nature of the impurities present must be taken into account. Similarly, not all coal will make coke. Indeed, but a minor part of the known coal in the world will yield this highly desirable metallurgical fuel. Coking coal is rare throughout the world, and this is true of the Far East as elsewhere.

So far as coal itself is concerned, China is well supplied. Indeed, that country contains one of the great coal reserves of the world. W. H. Wong and P. Y. Hu of the Geological Survey of China have but recently published a review of previous estimates of the coal reserves of China and presented revised figures of their own.

The first important consolidated estimates of China's coal reserves were made for the International Geological Congress and were presented at the Canadian meeting in 1913. Two sets of figures were presented, one by N. F. Drake, an American engineer long resident in China, and one by K. Inouyè, then director of the Geological Survey of Japan. Both estimates were confessedly approximations only. The totals differed strikingly. Drake, who had the wider acquaintance with the country, considered the probable reserve to be of the order of 996,613 million tons. Inouyè, who had the more accurate knowledge of certain provinces, gave a total of 39,565 million tons. Soon after the initial studies of the Geological Survey of China, V. K. Ting and W. H. Wong (1921) estimated the "actual" reserve at 213,255 million tons. In 1925, C. Y. Hsieh estimated the probable reserve as 217,623 million tons, of which 152,973 were credited to provinces as to which the Geological Survey had considerable data. The 1929 estimates of Wong and Hu place the total probable reserve at 265,455 million tons, of which 218,455 is credited to provinces at least moderately well known. In 1932, on the basis of survey in 23 provinces, the figure was slightly decreased by W. H. Wong and T. F. Hou, who gave 250,000 million tons as the best estimate then possible to be made. By way of comparison it may be stated that the reserves of the United States are of the order of 3,800,000 million tons; Canada, 800,000 million; Australia, 163,000 million; Japan, 8,000 million. In each case round figures are quoted. China ranks third among the nations of the world in coal reserves.

The record of coal exploration and mining in China has, however, been one of continuous disappointment and shrinkage in estimates. Accurate drilling or extensive underground work has repeatedly shown the amount of workable coal present to be very much less than would have been legitimately inferred from the outcrops. Variation in thickness, concealed faults, intrusions of igneous rocks, all these have been found to reduce the actual amount of coal from the expected. In specific instances this shrinkage has been of such order as from 150 million tons to 20 million tons. None the less, China does possess large amounts of excellent coal widely distributed and, despite the many difficulties to be overcome, it seems reasonably certain that one of the big coal-mining industries of the world will in time grow up within that country, with all that this implies in the way of supplementing human power with steam. All varieties of coal are present, and while as elsewhere in the world good coking coal forms but a minor fraction of the whole, the total amount available is large, particularly when contrasted with that found in other countries of the Far East.

Actual development of modern coal mining in China has been determined by accidents of foreign contact, native ambition, and other minor elements rather than by the sum of favorable geographic conditions. In Manchuria it was first the Russian need for railway fuel and later Japanese initiative that forced the pace and led to opening of the large mines at Fushun, Penhsihu, and elsewhere. In Jehol it was Chinese initiative and desire to offset foreign activities. At Tangshan, northeast of Tientsin, the Cantonese first opened modern mines at Kaiping, to be later joined by British and Belgian interests in building up the Kailan Mining Administration, which operates a most important group of large collieries. In Shantung the Germans led in modernizing and enlarging the small native mines, though control later passed to the Japanese or was recovered by Chinese. Along the mountain front west of Peiping and extending south into Honan a series of collieries have been opened by Chinese, or by Chinese working with British, German, Belgian, or other foreign groups. The interior position of the fields and the limited amount of local industry have retarded the growth of these collieries, despite the abundance and good quality of the coal present. In central and southern China there are a number of collieries of which the Pinghsiang in Kiangsi is the largest. These were opened mainly by Chinese, though in a number of instances they had the assistance of technical men and, in a few, foreign capital participated. The largest coal fields known in China, those of Shansi and Shensi, are as yet but little exploited save by small native mines, and contribute but a minor part to the annual output. Coal development on a modern scale both requires and generates industry, and in an agricultural region with household handicrafts supplying most of the manufactures, operating big coal mines successfully is contingent on a large degree of change in social structure.

The supplementary mineral fuels, petroleum and natural gas, have nowhere been found in quantity in China, and reasons connected with the geology of the country, backed by such drilling as has been done, have led specialists to the conclusion that the finding of large fields of either is highly improbable.

The second most important mineral resource in modern industry is iron ore, and here again resurvey of the Far East has led to revision downward of early expectations, except in the Philippines and Netherlands East Indies, where extensive deposits of lateritic ores have been found, and in India, where iron ore reserves of first rank are now known to be present. An excellent general survey and summary of the iron ore resources of the Far East, indeed of the whole Pacific basin, was made by F. R. Tegengren, an experienced engineer especially competent in this field, and has been published by the Geological Survey of China.

Tegengren showed that the Pacific countries are generally deficient in iron ore. Among them China has the largest potential resources and Japan among the smallest. Any large figure of tonnage from China, however, must be arrived at by including material of doubtful value, of grades not generally recognized elsewhere as commercial, and which can be utilized if at all only at a material increase of cost. Including all such deposits, Tegengren credits the country with an "actual," or more accurately a probable, workable reserve of 396 million tons of ore containing 166 million tons of metallic iron. To this he adds 555,200,000 tons of potential ore containing 202,200,000 tons of iron. Even these large figures correspond to about two tons only per capita, a very small reserve compared with that of the United States, where the corresponding amount is 670 tons. It is clear that even if China preserves for the use of its own people all its iron, and proves unusually fortunate in working low-grade material, the actual tonnage present is not nearly enough to permit development of an iron and steel industry such as has taken place in America, or the degree of industrialization that steel has made possible in the latter country. Japan is not even so well off, since the iron ore reserve in that country and under its control amounts to even less per capita.

Somewhat similar conditions exist in both countries

as regards most of the other important minerals. Japan contains important .copper mines, but even now sometimes imports and sometimes exports. China does not entirely satisfy even its present low per capita consumption requirements, and no deposits likely to change this condition for any long period have been found. Neither country contains the common non-ferrous minerals in sufficient amounts to furnish any large exportable surplus or to sustain extensive local industrialization, though as to particular minerals they may be moderately well supplied. Japan, for example, as a lead producer ranks with Canada.

China is the world's foremost producer of antimony and tungsten ores, and Japan produces and exports sulphur, though both as to quantity and ease of production its sulphur mines do not rank with the American sources in Louisiana and Texas. Neither China nor Japan is an important producer, from the world's point of view, of non-ferrous minerals, nor are any non-metallic resources known within their border likely to afford an exportable surplus corresponding with the nitrates in Chile or the phosphate rock of North Africa and the United States. When examined with care it becomes increasingly clear that if any major industrialization takes place in the Far East the region will necessarily become an importer of minerals and mineral products, with the exceptions already indicated. To these exceptions may be added tin in the Malay States and the Netherlands East Indies with smaller amounts in Siam, Burma, and elsewhere. Informed opinion now everywhere accepts this conclusion.

As has already been intimated, this has not been accepted until recently, and out of the older belief in a China exceptionally rich in all that goes to support modern industry, and with a hardy and industrious population, have arisen many false hopes and fears. Friction between China and the foreign powers has frequently had its origin in some project for development of mineral deposits which unfortunately are now known to have been not worth the effort. The whole French attempt to dominate Yunnan, including the building of a most difficult and expensive railway into the interior, was founded upon misconceptions of the geology of the country and a resulting mistaken belief in the size and value of the mineral deposits. William F. Collins, a British mining engineer stationed in China for some years to help settle the affairs of the Yunnan Syndicate, has written in detail the history of this and other foreign attempts to control the mines of China. It is one long record of disappointment arising in considerable part out of mistaken belief in the size or value of the individual deposits by foreigners, Chinese, or both.

After the French had obtained possession of Annam, Tonking was conquered as a result of objections of local authorities to the effort of a French merchant to export copper and tin from Yunnan in exchange for salt. In the treaty made in settlement with China in 1885 in which the French conquest of Tonking was recognized, provision was inserted requiring that in exploitation of mines in Yunnan, Kuangsi, and Kuantung the Chinese give preference to French commerce and engineers, and that the French railways be prolonged into the adjacent Chinese territory. When in fact such railways were projected, it was upon the basis of examinations of the territory by geologists and mining engineers, who presented a glowing picture of the wealth of the mines to be opened and served, including the expectation that the coal market at Hong Kong would be supplied by mines in Yunnan. Before the line was actually completed to Yunnan-fu, a resurvey by geologists more familiar with the region deflated these expectations, but there can be no doubt that the lure of the supposed mineral wealth of the region was one of the prime incentives of the French to their aggressive campaign in the Southwest.

North of this French "sphere of influence" and extending up through the Yangtze Kiang Valley an indefinite distance to the north was a similar sphere that the British marked out for themselves. In their activities trade ranked first, but they showed, none the less, a keenness hardly behind that of the French to acquire possession of such mines as were present. Perhaps the most famous of their efforts in this direction was that of the Eastern Pioneer company, founded on concessions obtained by Prichard Morgan through Li Hung Chang. This, with the Kiangpeiting concession of Archibald Little, had to do with mineral areas in Szechuan and led to long years of controversy with the Chinese. To the south conflict with the French as to mineral rights was ultimately quieted by the formation of the Yunnan Syndicate, an Anglo-French company which because of opposition of the local gentry was never able to accomplish any development of importance.

In the Yangtze Kiang Valley proper the Anhui Concession of Sir John Lester Kaye, covering the Tung Kuan Shan iron mine and financed by the London and

China Syndicate, may be mentioned as one which again resulted only in long-drawn-out controversy and bad feeling. Among the most important, however, of the British attempts to mine was that of the Pekin Syndicate. The concession on which this was founded was obtained in 1898 by an Italian, Comandatore Angelo Luzatti. It was financed and controlled in London and covered mining, ironworks, and transportation of mine products of all kinds in the province of Shansi, then supposed to be one of the richest coal and iron fields of the world, together with that part of Honan that lies north of the Yellow River. This concession aroused great opposition among the people, and after expert examination had determined that the iron ores were of little or no value, the Shansi rights were ceded back by the British on payment of a substantial sum by the Chinese. Collieries were, however, opened in Honan, and a ninety-mile railway, which was later sold to the Chinese government, was built. Attempts to construct an extensive system of railways, extending even to Pukow opposite Nanking, under a clause permitting construction of "railways to connect with other railways and with water navigation," was successfully opposed by the Chinese.

In North China the most important British venture into mining came when, at the time of the Boxer Rebellion, the Kaiping collieries northeast of Tientsin were transferred to the British flag. A substantial Belgian interest was created at the same time, and these mines became the nucleus of the present Kailan Mining Administration, in which were merged after much controversy British, Belgian, and Chinese interests. Until the rise of the Fushun collieries this was the largest mining enterprise in the Far East and it has long been one of the most successful. Out of the need of an outlet to the sea for the Kaiping mines grew what is now the Peking-Mukden Railway and the opening of Chingwangtao, an ice-free port on the Gulf of Pechili.

German adventures in China were not behind those of France and England in the importance attached to the control of the mines. As early as 1887 Baron von Richthofen had called attention to the value of the coal fields of Shantung and had suggested that a railway extending from Kiaochao to Peking could be made the basis of control of the supply of coal in northern waters. Ten years later the Germans made their dramatic descent upon the bay mentioned and proceeded to put into execution the plan envisaged by Von Richthofen. In the demands made upon China at that time and later embodied in a treaty between the two nations was the right not only to build the projected Shantung railways but "to work any mine which may exist along the track of such railway." The Shantung Mining Company was promptly organized and was used to make this right effective as well as to prevent the Chinese from independently modernizing their mines.

German technical skill was employed to open a number of modern collieries, now in Japanese or Sino-Japanese hands, and at the opening of the World War the Germans were planning to open the Chinlingchen iron mines and to build a blast furnace near Tsingtao. Fortunately for German investors the latter project was not far advanced when the war broke. The Japanese, after they succeeded to possession of the German rights,

pushed vigorously in the direction of dominating coal-
mining in the province, but after examination of the
iron mines allowed the blast furnace project to lapse.
The Germans were also responsible for opening the
Ching Hsing coal mines west of Peking, though in this
instance it was organized as a Sino-German concern.
Yuan Shi Kai, resenting the pressure the Germans had
put upon the government to secure the concession,
caused the Ching Hsing Bureau to be organized as a
competitive enterprise in the same field. After a period
of disastrous competiton the two were merged on terms
satisfactory to the Chinese. This method of forcing
readjustment of the terms of a concession has been
used repeatedly by the Chinese.

Belgian mining enterprise, aside from the interest
held by Belgians in the Kailan mines, has found its field
mainly along the Pekin-Hankow Railway and may be
regarded as in the main an effort to secure fuel for that
system. At one time Belgians directed the Lincheng,
Tzecheng and Liuhokow mines, in all of which the
Chinese were partners. Relatively little friction developed out of Belgian participation in mining, and
their interests have now largely been liquidated.

Russian interests in mines in China have been naturally confined to Mongolia and Manchuria. It was Von
Grot, a Russian, who made a success of Mongolor, an
important gold-mining undertaking near Urga, in
which Chinese, Mongols, and Russians at the time
had interests. In Manchuria the Russians pioneered
modern mining as well as railway building and at one
time, as a result of the Cassini convention of 1896 and
supplementary treaties, they held, at least on paper,

dominant rights in mining over most of Manchuria. Actually little beyond exploration was accomplished except in the opening of the Fushun and Yentai collieries, which under subsequent Japanese control have become large and successful. The Fushun Colliery now ranks both in reserve and output among the great mining enterprises of the world. Russian progress in mining in China was stopped by the Russo-Japanese War, and what remaining rights Russia held were lost with extraterritoriality at the close of the World War.

Japanese attempts to mine in China have been frankly connected with movements to dominate the country politically as well as commercially. Japanese have little or no faith in the ability or willingness of the Chinese to police their own territory and so provide the peace and order necessary to the conduct of large mining enterprises. Japanese also, having come quickly out of feudalism into a highly industrialized world, have had neither a large nor a long established merchant class to fight for private as against government control of enterprises, and they turn naturally to the government for initiative and support. Japanese, too, have had longer experience and have shown higher skill in organization and conduct of government than of industry, and it is not unnatural that back of their attempts to open and operate mines in their neighbors' territory there has been usually a national purpose and a national power, disguised thinly, if at all. A few exceptions occur, and private firms have played a part, though a relatively small one. The Okura firm took the lead in financing and directing the Penshihu Sino-Japanese coal and iron enterprise in Manchuria and in the attempt to secure possession of the Feng Huan Shan iron mines near Nanking. The loans which form the basis of the claims of the Japanese upon the Hanyangping company were made mainly by the Yokohama Specie Bank, though the Industrial Bank of Japan made the first and the Nippon Yusen Kaisha also participated. The pig iron and ore received in payment have gone largely to the government steel works at Yawata. Aside from the Penshihu mines, the South Manchurian Railway, a semi-government corporation, is the dominant owner and operator of mines in Manchuria. It succeeded to the ownership of the Russian rights in the Fushun and Yentai coal deposits and to those in six additional districts secured by the Japanese as a result of the famous Twenty-one Demands in 1915. These included four coal fields, one of coal and iron, and one of gold. Less definite rights in various other deposits were acquired prior to the recent conquest of Manchuria and Jehol, since which they have come into practical possession of all the mineral wealth of the area, whatever may be the exact legal status of title as regards particular properties.

Exactly how significant this possession will prove to be remains in part to be seen. Their reserves of coal available have been notably increased, and the ability of the Japanese to handicap the Chinese in competition for the coal markets of the Far East has been hardly less notably augmented. A very large portion of the estimated iron ore reserves of China lies within the area occupied. The ore is of the Archean type, and according to the estimate of Tegengren, 740,000,000 tons out of 772,000,000 credited to this type in China lie within the area. The Japanese, in fact, now control something over

[205]

80 percent of the iron ore reserves of China as estimated by Tegengren. It is not so certain, however, that these particular "reserves" are of as great value as these figures suggest. Out of the whole Tegengren found but 6,300,000 tons of high-grade ore; that is, of ore sufficiently rich in iron to be used in the furnace without beneficiation. The remainder is of such low quality that but little would be taken into calculation of reserves in any other country. The Japanese have devoted much time and money at Anshan to the problem of so concentrating the ore as to make it suitable for the furnace. The problem is one which is capable of technical solution, but whether an economically sound answer can be found is still doubtful. In any event, the use of these ores will be at additional cost and will operate as a handicap to Manchurian blast furnaces.

Aside from coal and iron, Manchuria and Mongolia contain numerous deposits of the common non-ferrous metals, but up to now none of large size have been developed. Gold is found both in quartz mines and in placers, and in northern Manchuria in particular there are distinct possibilities of the finding of placers of considerable value. Heretofore the region has been too inaccessible and too bandit infested to permit of careful study. Neither Manchuria nor Jehol is known to contain oil or gas fields and for much of the area the geological factors are unfavorable to their presence. At Fushun large amounts of oil shale are present and must be removed in mining coal. Extensive experimental work has been done on them and a plant of moderate size has been erected to recover the oil and by-products. This has been financed by sales to the navy and must be regarded still as more a war than an industrial enterprise.

While many other factors have entered into the situation, there can be no doubt that aggressive action of the Japanese in China, including war and conquest, has been to a considerable degree founded upon the desire, and assumed necessity, to obtain possession of mineral deposits, especially coal and iron. One needs only to read the Twenty-one Demands or indeed to study the revised map, to assure himself of this. The result so far has been to bring under the control of the Japanese a large and excellent coal supply and a large supply of iron ore that can be used in case of necessity but which is of doubtful commercial importance. A correlative result has been to weaken by so much the Chinese, though as to coal they still possess one of the great world reserves. But it is also to be remembered that in taking over Manchuria, population as well as resources came under Japanese domination. In any use that may be made of the mineral wealth of the region, the needs of the local population will necessarily be taken into account.

A friendly outsider can but feel that the Japanese have made a conquest at heavy cost and of doubtful value so far as gain in possession of mineral wealth is concerned. The important iron ore deposits, such as they are, were already under their financial control and management. Possession of the connecting railway lines assured them outlet. The leading, and in particular the most important, coal mine was already securely theirs, and the reserves were ample. While the coal lacked coking quality, it was useful even in this field for admixture. The spread of Japanese armies over all Manchuria and Jehol has notably increased the coal reserve under Japan's control, but it is by no means certain that this will result in corresponding profit. There are important competitive mines, such as those of the Kailan mining administration, so situated as to be able to play a large part in setting the price of coal in the competitive field. Unless Japan is prepared to challenge England and Belgium as well as China, or to come to terms with them, this competition cannot be blotted out. In Japan, the domestic mines already protest development of those of Manchuria at their own expense. Coal mining is a business which is usually conducted on a small margin of profit per ton, and while that has not heretofore been true in the Far East the abundance of coal would seem to indicate it as inevitable in the future. One wonders whether astute business negotiation would not have brought about adequate participation by the Japanese in coal development without necessity for payment of heavy taxes to amortize the cost of the military adventures of the past two years.

So far as minerals other than coal and iron are concerned, there is no satisfactory evidence that they exist either in Manchuria or Jehol in amounts even remotely commensurate to the inevitable cost of the Japanese adventure in those provinces. Any justification of the move must clearly be based upon other expected profits than from the mines.

American participation in mining in China has been minor. At times Americans have owned shares in various mining companies, native or foreign, and American engineers and machinery have found a limited employment. The Standard Oil Company of New York, in coöperation with the Chinese government, conducted the most extensive actual exploration for petroleum that has been undertaken. After expending a considerable sum under direction of experienced engineers the company withdrew, having found the yield of the wells put down too small to encourage hope of finding petroleum in quantity sufficient to support the pipe lines, refinery, and other facilities necessary to make a commercial success. Various American companies or syndicates have examined particular deposits and in a few instances have done a small amount of mining, but nothing warranting extensive work has been found. Perhaps the most ambitious exploration was that conducted by the New York Orient Mines Company, which kept a well equipped staff in the field from 1916 to 1922 and made examinations in many provinces. It also did initial work directed toward reopening certain ancient mines in Yunnan. Eventually the staff was withdrawn, as the prospect of finding and working metal mines on the necessary scale was considered too discouraging to warrant further expenditure.

The long record of failure of foreign mining enterprises in China and of steady opposition to them on the part of the Chinese warrants a few words of general explanation. As has already been indicated, careful and competent exploration has very generally proved the deposits to be disappointingly small or low in grade. It is to be remembered that a foreign company can hardly maintain the necessary staff and import the machinery incident to modern mining unless the enterprise itself is so large that the overhead cost may be distributed over an adequate tonnage. The truth is that of the mineral deposits of China, such as those of tungsten which are notable, the greater part are individually small and are better adapted to operation by Chinese than by foreign companies.

Belief in the size or richness of a mineral deposit is a common fallacy of landowners. The less such an owner knows about mining, the more he is apt to be deceived by his ignorance of mining risks and mining costs. It is not surprising therefore that the Chinese, both the people and the various governments, have commonly overestimated the value of such deposits as are present and have asked impossible terms for their development. They have often looked upon those who wished to mine as virtual robbers, and in fairness it must be said that concession hunters have by no means always offered just terms. A more prolific cause for friction has been that the various contracts entered into have been vaguely drawn through carelessness, ignorance, or with a purpose, and often promises have been made which were entirely impossible of fulfillment on any business basis. Add to this the differences in language, institutions, and laws, and controversy was certain to arise.

One of the most reasonable objections which Chinese have had to extensive mining by foreigners within the country is the existence of extraterritoriality. Under that system a miner or a mining company, if allowed to go into the interior, took the foreign laws with him and as a practical matter it was impossible for Chinese authorities, however willing, to administer under such conditions with foreigners established throughout the country. Conflict has been common enough even with the foreigners restricted to a few treaty ports. Where foreign companies have been willing to accept Chinese jurisdiction and Chinese as real partners, it has been possible to negotiate fair terms. With all these possible sources of friction, it is not surprising that the attempt of foreigners to mine in China has been generally looked upon by the Chinese as a struggle to get possession of a mine as a means of possessing the country. The broader and more exact knowledge now available regarding the deposits should remove much of such incentive where it has existed among the foreign nations and should profoundly influence their policies.

At the beginning it was pointed out that the bringing into contact of two different cultures, one old and based upon exploitation of but a limited portion of the earth's forces and products, and another young, vigorous, and with proved technique for control of a much larger number of materials and forces, inevitably presaged conflict. It was also indicated that the most important difference between the peoples of the two regions was in the degrees in which they used minerals and the energy created by them. It has been seen how, in the push into China of the British, French, Germans, Americans, Japanese, and others, there has been underlying always the desire to possess or control the development of the supposed great mineral wealth of the country. It is now clear that there was more supposition than wealth in this long current idea; that China, and the Far East generally, except for coal and a few minor specialties, is deficient rather than rich in mineral wealth; that if a great industrial civilization of the same type as our own develops in the Far East the latter must be an importer rather than an exporter of minerals; and, finally, that owing to poverty of such mineral resources and the inherent difficulties in their utilization the West has nothing to fear from the East in competition based upon them. The relation might well be instead rather one of mutual benefit. The Far East has a surplus of tin, antimony, arsenic, and a few minor but important minerals. As a whole, and this is particularly true of China, it has adequate coal with which to work up local materials both mineral and vegetable, and to reprocess to advantage crude or semi-finished imports. It has the basis for an important but not dominating chemical industry which is now rising in Japan. The Netherlands East Indies, Sakhalin, and possibly other regions, can be expected to make important contributions to the most wonderful of modern fuels, petroleum. The Far East does not have the ores basic to such industrialization as has marked the countries bordering the North Atlantic through the last half century, and the full development of such as it has constitutes no threat to the rest of the world. The basis of the conflict which has been waged is false so far as concerns minerals themselves—the backbone of the modern industrial development of the West.

THE STRUGGLE FOR FOOD

THE STRUGGLE FOR FOOD
Carl L. Alsberg

Ever since the first Western traders sailed into the Pacific, food and the products of agriculture, as well as commerce, banking, and the minerals of the earth, have bulked very large in the intercourse between East and West. To the early desire for spices and tea, there has been added the modern demand of industry for raw silk, camphor, and rubber. The vegetable oil of soya beans and coconuts, fruits and nuts, cacao beans, sugar, and rice all appear among the imports of the United States from the Pacific region, and their relative importance in the total of American imports has steadily grown. Modern empires in the Pacific, whether colonial or commercial, have some of their deepest roots in the struggle for food and other products of the soil.

As these empires have grown, significant changes have been brought about both in the motivation of this struggle and in the conditions under which it has taken place. Shifts in the pressure of population upon food resources and new technical discoveries have profoundly altered in the last hundred years both the nature of the Western demand for agricultural wealth from the East and the ability of the East to produce it. The colonial policies of Western empires are effective today in the measure in which they have been adjusted to these important changes.

Among very primitive peoples still in the earliest stages of development, the struggle for food is a struggle against the elements, against pests and wild beasts. Drought and flood take such heavy toll of the harvest that primitive man, except under very favorable circumstances, always faces the risk of starvation. It matters little if he does not suffer from failure of the food supply each year; catastrophes, though occurring at long intervals, may nevertheless set a limit to population growth. It is not so much the average environment that determines the fate of primitive man as its extremes. In an otherwise favorable environment, a single typhoon that destroys most of the coconut palms of an island, a single crop failure from whatever cause that decimates a tribe, a single year's absence of the spawning migration of salmon may suffice to check population growth for many years.

This is the situation which prevailed in all agricultural regions of the western Pacific so long as transportation was inadequate and purchasing power low. It prevails even today in many sections of China, where an old and highly developed farming tradition has not protected Chinese peasants from the sudden and ravaging incidence of flood or other catastrophe. Where wealth has become greater and communications better, as in

Japan, the crisis of famine has now become a crisis of finance. Moving foodstuffs to stricken areas may load upon governments great financial burdens and lead to serious economic dislocations. In other areas of the Pacific, and particularly in those whose products, often of a tropical nature, are exported, and where at the same time the native lives on a level close to the lowest possible for subsistence, this factor is still more important. The native might get food from abroad, but he lacks reserve of purchasing power.

Isolated catastrophes may be disastrous under such conditions because transport is lacking. Primitive man cannot bring in food from a distance. Moreover, he is rarely able to store up adequate reserves, either because the technique of producing food is so imperfect that it does not provide a sufficient surplus over and above the maintenance ration of those engaged in its production, or because of the perishability of foodstuffs, or both. Perishable food must be preserved in some manner if it is to be stored as a reserve; but methods of preservation were not always known. This difficulty arises especially in the warm, moist portions of the world, for warmth and dampness favor decay. Moreover, tropical foods tend to be even more perishable than those of cool climates. Thus corn (maize), the principal grain of the American tropics, and rice, the principal grain of the Old World tropics, keep less well than barley, wheat, and rye. It is not without reason that manioc (cassava) is spreading through the tropics. Not only does it yield a very large amount of food to the unit of land and of labor, but the crop need not all be harvested at once; being both a tuber and a perennial it may be garnered for immediate consumption from time to time as needed. Moreover, it may easily be converted into such imperishable products as cakes, starch, and tapioca.

In the early stages of the evolution of agricultural peoples the limiting factor in the struggle for food was, therefore, not land. Recurring disasters from drought, flood, hurricane, and frost, rather than lack of land, held down numbers. Population remained sparse, and the problem of soil exhaustion was met simply by moving the fields from place to place as crop yields fell. The worn-out cultivated field was then left to itself and regained its fertility in the course of years, if it was not destroyed by erosion or made untillable by the growth of some weed like the cogon grass of the Philippine Islands. In temperate zones this type of farming took the form of fallowing, and it has lasted in Europe well into recent times. Indeed, there are many regions in which it is still practised. In the humid tropics such as are found in southeastern Asia, we find instead of the fallow the clearing in the jungle, known in Malay as *ladang* and in the Philippine Islands as *kaingin*. The native, when a clearing has been exhausted, makes a fresh one in a new part of the jungle by burning off the trees and brush, and plants it to crops until it too in turn is exhausted, whereupon he moves to a fresh piece of jungle or to an old clearing that has grown up to jungle and recovered its fertility. An analogous practice is still found in the northern part of the Scandinavian Peninsula. Where this type of agriculture predominates, most of the land seems to be idle and to belong to no one, whereas, in fact, the villagers have the customary right to use it for *ladang* or *kaingin*, or for some corresponding purpose.

The land is therefore by no means no man's land but the common land of all the villagers.

The hazards of the elements through the limitations they impose upon the food supply are not the only factors that check numbers: wars, disorders, and disease are also important. In spite of all, population increases in time both because of improvements in technique and because of changes in social organization that ensure at least some degree of peace and order and, ultimately, some betterment of sanitation. Farming becomes more efficient, floods are controlled by waterworks, droughts are combated by irrigation, new crops are discovered or borrowed from other tribes, strong rulers or governments arise, and so on. Then population increases more rapidly till in the end it is no longer merely the elements but also the scarcity of land that limits the local food supply.

In the past, this stage has been reached in the course of centuries; indeed, many races have not yet achieved it. In the nineteenth century, a new factor appeared: the colonizing white man. In some regions, he introduced disease or unwise administration or exploitation, which checked population increase, as, for example, in certain Pacific islands. In other regions, conditions were not favorable for the spread of the white man's diseases, and there peace, order, and above all sanitation imposed by colonial administrators caused the population to increase by leaps and bounds. Thus, the population of Java increased from between three and four millions in 1815 to thirty-five millions in 1925. In many places, the white man played the rôle of dry nurse to the blacks and browns. There tens of millions live their span who but for the white man's technology and police would never have been born.

In the meanwhile, before technology, peace and sanitation have had time to achieve their full effects upon population numbers, the colonial power often grants the apparently ownerless land in freehold or on long leases to planters. It does so either in ignorance of the customary ancient interest of natives in the land or in deliberate disregard of his rights. So long as the population has not multiplied much, all goes well. Soon, however, the land begins to be filled up. The time may come when the native has not enough land to produce the food he needs for his subsistence. He has to give up practising fallowing or making his *ladang* or his *kaingin*. He begins to eye the planter's land as the French peasant must have looked upon the lands of the lord of the manor before the Revolution.

In the colonial offices of European governments there are two schools of thought regarding the type of colonial policy best suited to prevent this state of affairs. One school believes that it is the part of wisdom not to develop a backward colony too rapidly by encouraging exploitation with Western capital through the establishment of plantations, the development of mines, or the felling of forests. It seeks to discourage the alienation of land. It seeks to encourage the native as rapidly as possible to exploit his own country's natural resources rather than to have them exploited for him by imported capital. Its ultimate goal is to develop the native into an independent land-owning farmer and to preserve such portions of the indigenous culture as may be compatible with a monetary economy in a competitive world. It believes that in the long run the mother country will profit immensely, for there will be created a loyal population with a reasonably high standard of living that will require immense quantities of manufactured goods in exchange for agricultural and other raw materials. It believes that the interests of the native peoples ought to come first, even if they run counter to what is economically profitable for the mother country.

The other school regards this as a beautiful but idle dream. It objects that development will be infinitely slow because development requires capital. It points out that the standard of living of the native is so low that the accumulation of the necessary capital must take almost infinite time. Because the income of the native is so small there is little to tax, and the colonial government cannot raise abundant revenues. It is, therefore, unable to build roads or railroads, maintain schools, public health services, or an adequate system for the administration of justice. It is doubtful whether the standard of living of the native can be raised in any reasonable length of time. In the meanwhile the colony must remain an ever increasing burden upon the treasury of the mother country.

A better plan, says this school of thought, is to pour capital into the country by establishing plantations, even if land must be alienated, and by exploiting mines, and forests, even if natural resources are used up. Then there will be something to tax, and revenue will be available to build roads and pay doctors and school teachers; there will be freight for railroads; there will be employment for native labor, and the standard of living will go up; there will be an increasing market for manufactured goods. The benefit to the native will not be postponed to the distant future.

All this the first school of thought admits, but it believes the price the native has to pay is too high. Rapid development it regards as undesirable if the ultimate result is to make the native a landless agricultural laborer or a proletarian factory worker.

Furthermore, they point out that where there are plantations with European management, the native tends to learn only what he is taught as a plantation laborer. This may not be what would help him to improve his own farming technology. He continues to practise his traditional subsistence farming, that is, each family produces all, or nearly all, that it needs. Efficiency in production is low, for the efficiency that comes from division of labor and exchange of products is lacking. The native tends only slowly to raise his efficiency and productivity through specialization which has been at the bottom of most forms of national progress in the last century or more. He continues to grow his food crops whether or not his land is better suited to the production of some other crop, which he might sell for more than enough to cover the purchase of what he needs. The standard of living remains low, for he is ordinarily unable to produce a surplus for sale, and in consequence there is little left over his subsistence needs with which to raise his own standard of living, except possibly what he may achieve as a worker upon near-by plantations.

One cannot, if one keeps in mind the consequences to the native, object if the establishment of large plantations is discouraged and the size of land-holdings is limited where an indigenous people retains control over land policy, as in the Philippine Islands. The Dutch have come to similar conclusions, for they no longer permit any agricultural land to be alienated. Indeed, in Java they are buying back, as the colonial finances permit, land which was alienated in former times. Such land, formerly alienated, is relatively small in area and lies principally in sultanates, the administration of which has only very recently been taken over by the Dutch government. Except for this land, all the plantations are on land leased from the villages for short terms under conditions largely fixed by the government. It can therefore be turned back to the native should circumstances require it.

The Japanese have not been so wise in their dependencies. In Korea, no effective steps were taken, when it passed under Japanese control, to safeguard the interests of the ignorant, improvident Koreans who are inexperienced in business dealings. By perfectly legal means, a very large proportion of the land has passed very naturally into the hands of capitalists, and the Korean peasant has been reduced very largely to the status of an agricultural laborer. This seems always to happen when a backward, ignorant peasantry, which has hardly become acquainted with a monetary system, comes in contact with advanced, progressive business men, who have capital at their disposal. We see the same thing among the poor whites and black tenant farmers of some of our own Southern states. The end is always trouble, and the Japanese, in the agrarian unrest which they are now facing in Korea, are paying the penalty of lack of foresight in protecting their new Korean subjects from the loss of their lands. In a similar manner, China is in a measure paying the penalty for the action in years gone by of her own officials in Manchuria who managed to gain possession in fee simple of large tracts of unoccupied crown lands. The result is that of the thirty million Chinese who went to Manchuria, a very large proportion went under what amounts to a system of labor recruiting which settled them on these crown lands, nominally as tenant farmers, but actually as little more than agricultural laborers with scant hope of ever achieving land-ownership or economic independence. Had the Manchurian land policy been such as to favor the establishment there of a sturdy, independent, pioneer community in the North American sense, the Manchurian question of today might, perhaps, have a different complexion.

In China itself, the large and possibly growing degree of tenancy has produced problems which are not simply agricultural but which affect the entire political destiny of that country. It is a curious fact, and one of significance to the whole problem of land alienation in the agricultural regions of the Pacific, that the Soviet districts of central China appear to have developed and flourished in just those areas where the percentage of tenant farmers is highest. An independent, land-owning peasantry, no matter what its standard of living, is less likely to revolt than a community of tenants leasing their fields from absent landlords.

Elsewhere in the Pacific, the colonizing white man has brought results which differ widely. In the Philippines, the United States has left the land policy largely to the Island Legislature. The public domain is not being alienated in large tracts, but in small homesteads of from twelve to sixteen hectares. While these tracts would be too small to support a family in the United States, it must be remembered that the growing season is continuous, and more intensive agriculture than in cool climates is necessary. In consequence of this policy there is a considerable internal migration in the Islands, and true pioneering.

Finally, in Siberia and in central Asia, the Soviet Union is attempting to work out a new answer to this problem. The opening up of new agricultural lands in these areas is being carried on through socialized, collective farming. It is too early to appraise the results of this policy even in European Russia. When it is applied to the Asiatic portions of the U. S. S. R., where agricultural extension is complicated by problems of irrigation, transport, and markets, its possibilities are still to be learned.

The three most important factors that enter into agricultural production, that is, farming, are, as everyone knows, capital, labor, and land. The greatest efficiency is achieved, of course, when these three factors are combined in the optimum proportions relative to their prices. To use any one of them alone as *the* criterion by which farming efficiency may be gauged leads to serious misconceptions. If we employ the return per unit of land which we call yield as our criterion, we must hold that form of farming most efficient which yields the most per acre; if, on the contrary, our criterion is labor, we must hold that form of farming most efficient which yields the most per hour of labor. It is often assumed that the most efficient form of farming is that which produces the most per unit of land sometimes called intensive farming. However, as we have seen, intensive farming is efficient in only one respect —use of land. It is usually rather inefficient by our last criterion, labor, for intensive farming is mostly characterized by the application of a great deal of labor to each unit of land.

Moreover, it does not follow that wherever much labor is applied to the land, farming is especially efficient with respect either to labor or to land. This is not necessarily the case. Farming without good tools or good technique may give low yields, even though the amount of labor used is large. The rice yields of Java and of much of China are comparatively low, despite the large amount of labor employed. One practically never sees weeds in a Java *sawah* (irrigated rice field). They are carefully pulled up by hand. One sees many weeds in a California rice field, which is plowed, seeded, and harvested by machinery, yet the yields are much higher than in Java, though the man-labor hours per unit area are very much less in California than in Java. The highest rice yields in the world are found in Spain and not in China. Japan, which produces rice by intensive methods, in that it employs much labor and little machinery, is among the high-rice-yield countries, not because its methods are intensive, but because it has applied modern science with phenomenal success to the increasing of rice yields. In the last forty years, average yields for the country have almost doubled. The same results could undoubtedly be achieved in China and in Java. Chinese experts believe that yields could be increased 20 to 30 per cent at least, merely by systematic selection of the best strains of existing varieties. How much further yields might be improved by the scientific breeding of new varieties, no one can say. In Java, rice yields are kept low, in part because fertilizer is not used. Phosphate is especially needed, and it has been demonstrated that by its use alone yields can be increased materially. China is always held up as the country which uses every last bit of fertilizer material available. While this is probably true, it is not justifiable to assume that in consequence fertilization is intense and heavy, taking the country as a whole. On the contrary, there is reason to believe that by and large the quantities of fertilizer used are far below the optimum, and that the application of larger amounts, were they available, would lead to very material increase in yields.

The Chinese and the Javanese peasant should not be criticized too hastily for failure to adopt new methods, or to specialize in agricultural production. Very likely, he is quite as quick to see where he can make a profit as anyone else. Very generally, if a man refuses to change his ways, it is because he fails to see the benefit in such a change. Or it may be that the change involves capital outlays, or what comes to the same thing, the storage and holding of products which he, the peasant, practically lacking capital, is not in a position to make. To purchase fertilizer necessitates having a certain amount of capital or credit at one's disposal. The system of credit in the Dutch East Indies is an organized, governmental credit system, but in China there is none. How devoid of capital is the Javanese peasant is evidenced by the fact that the principal credit system is the government pawnshop, the average loan of which is less than five guilders (less than $2.00 gold). The cooperative village banks in Java average loans of less than twenty-five guilders. In China, there is no well organized governmental credit system of any kind. The peasant and tenant farmer have difficulty in getting credit except at prohibitive rates. It is physically impossible for them to undertake the introduction of improved agricultural methods, if capital outlays or advances are involved. A crying need of rural primitive communities is a good, reasonable credit system, not for the landlord or the owner of estates, but for the poor peasant, the agricultural laborer, and the tenant farmer. Such a system must be adjusted to furnishing credits of merely a few dollars. It is one of the crying needs of the Filipino *tao*. It is one of the surest ways of protecting a poor peasant from exploitation by the landlord or village storekeeper.

It is often said that it is the native's own fault if he does not accumulate capital. When he is charged with improvidence, one will realize that this charge is often unjustifiable, if one keeps in mind the psychology of saving. Saving means present sacrifice and foregoing the satisfaction of a want or need with the expectation thereby of satisfying a need in the future. Therefore, whether or not anyone—white, black, yellow, red, or brown—saves, depends on the felt intensity of the present need in comparison with the future need. It is this ratio which, though imponderable, determines whether one saves. It follows that the lower the standard of living of the individual, the less is he likely to save, for the simple reason that his present wants will be the more intense, the less he has at the moment. A coolie, who with his family is never quite full fed, when through some good fortune he finds himself in possession of a few cents, can hardly be expected to lay by for the future. To satisfy his present hunger and gorge himself to repleteness is more natural than it would be for him to save his coppers in anticipation of the day, some time in the distant future, when he may be hungrier than he is in the present.

It is thus obvious that one of the factors in the struggle for food is the command of capital, but lack of capital also determines what land is arable. It is commonly believed that in a densely populated country like China every possible bit of land is producing crops. Nothing could be farther from the truth. The arability of a given piece of land depends not merely upon its fertility but also upon the amount of capital it is deemed worth while to apply to it. In subsistence farming, the peasant can cultivate only that land which with his primitive technique will yield enough food to maintain a family. If his technique is limited to the use of the spade or the hoe, the land must be rich enough to yield sufficient to support a family on an area which the farmer with his family can cultivate with these tools. Under these conditions, the only land that can be cultivated is the richest land, for only the richest land will yield enough to support a family on the small tract a family can spade or hoe. When the farmer accumulates enough capital to acquire a draft animal—an ox, a cow, a donkey, or a horse—that can be made to pull a plow, he is able to cultivate a somewhat larger piece of land, and, therefore, is able to support a family on poorer land than he could if he had no draft animal. If, instead of an ox and a wooden plow, he has enough capital to acquire several span of horses, a steel plow, and other horse-driven cultivating and harvesting machines, he can cultivate a still larger tract and produce enough food to support a family on still poorer land. And finally, if he has the capital to acquire power machinery, he can make a living on quite poor land, if need be.

In much of eastern Asia the farmers are so lacking in capital that they can make a living only on the very best land, and wide stretches of poorer lands, that would be regarded as arable in other countries, remain untouched, perhaps producing timber or scrub for firewood, for the high price of fuel in some parts of China permits of a rather considerable return from such land. There are therefore stretches of land which are potentially available for cultivation could the farmers accumulate sufficient capital. Undoubtedly the failure of the eastern Asiatic to develop an extensive form of farming, employing much land, much capital in the form of tools, draft animals, and machinery, but relatively little labor, has been an important factor in directing migration. Migration has had of necessity to be directed toward those areas where there was much rich land; it has had to avoid all other regions, leaving them to the nomad pastoralist. With the introduction of extensive methods it is to be expected that many a region now sparsely inhabited will become the seat of a considerable agricultural population.

The culture of rice by irrigation has also tended to

cause the neglect of non-irrigated crops. It is dry land crops that are primarily suited to extensive agriculture. Rice is peculiarly well adapted to cultivation without the application of power, either in the form of tools wielded by man, or of draft animals. A rice field may be flooded and the ground worked merely by trampling around on it. It is still sometimes the practice not to plow a rice field at all but to flood it and drive a carabao around and around until the entire field has been puddled. The rice itself is not sown in the field, but in a small, specially prepared seedbed, from which the seedlings are uprooted and planted one by one in the field, the workers standing ankle deep in water. Rice growers depend so exclusively on the single crop that they tend to neglect unirrigated crops. With infinite labor they terrace mountains and hillsides, even though there be available wide stretches of non-irrigable land suitable for dry crops. This has led, in Java, with the coming of the white man, to the stratification of agriculture. On the lowlands, rice and sugar and tobacco are grown under irrigation. A little higher up, above the levels of the ditches, coffee plantations or other tropical tree crops may begin, such as rubber or cacao. And above these, at higher elevations, there is tea. Still higher, approaching the frost line, there may be quinine. These tree crops are mostly cultivated in European plantations on land which was not formerly required by the Javanese, because he grew primarily irrigated crops and especially rice. There was, therefore, little or no competition for the land between the native and the planter except in the case of sugar, and to some extent tobacco. The native grew rice under irrigation and perhaps also leased some of his land to the sugar planter. The planter grew coffee, rubber, cacao, tea, and quinine on the hillsides which the native was unable to cultivate. With the increasing density of native population, this situation must ultimately change. The native may finally be driven to need the unirrigated lands. At present, where the water is ample, he grows two crops of rice a year on the same *sawah*. Where the water is adequate for only one rice crop, he is beginning to grow an additional crop in the dry season, such as maize, peanuts, beans, sweet potatoes. The outcome may ultimately be that the land is devoted almost wholly to the production of food for the natives, and the exportation of raw materials theretofore produced on the plantations may have to cease. The effects upon the commerce and industry of the home countries are obvious.

If the colonial types of country now exporting raw materials like rubber, sisal, manila hemp, coffee, tea, manioc, camphor, sugar, cacao, copra, peanuts, palm oil, and palm-kernel oil are one by one to curtail their exports because they have become so populous that all of their lands are required to raise foodstuffs, if they are ultimately to become Chinas teeming with millions who tax domestic agricultural production merely to be fed, this is important for the rest of the world to know. It would mean a gradual but continuous shifting in the sources of raw materials as country after country drops out of world trade. It might even mean ultimately a scarcity of some raw materials—at least in the distant future. However, such shifts have already taken place. For example, British India and Java were once important exporters of copra and coconut oil. They now consume most of their own production.

While developments like these are perhaps in the lap of the distant future, it is nevertheless worth while at least to discuss what are the factors that might prevent these countries from becoming self-contained economic units with but a small share in world trade and a low standard of living. If the advancement of the standard of living in these countries can be moderately rapid, there is every reason to believe that the native would ultimately lessen his rate of increase, for this has happened or is happening where the standard of living is relatively high. We need not concern ourselves here with the question why this is so or by what means the reduction of the birth rate is brought about. It is clearly, in the long run, in the interest of colonial powers to strain every effort to raise the native's standard of living rather than to exploit him. This means no alienation of land, the kind of education that will make of him a better farmer rather than a poor imitation of a white collar worker, an appropriate rural credit system, and, above all, the creation of a middle class which is usually lacking in these countries.

The civilized industrial man, whether white or yellow, in spreading his empire over the vast agricultural regions of the Pacific, has created for himself other problems which must eventually, if they have not already done so, affect vitally the character and the strength of that empire. For world commerce has achieved an interrelation between the rubber of the Malay States and the automobile industry of Detroit, between the quinine of Java and health in malarial lowlands, and between the tin mines of Siam or the Dutch East Indies and the dinner tables of America.

The problems which arise from this relationship transcend agricultural terms; they involve trade and tariffs, foreign exchange and depression. But they have introduced to the lives of millions of agricultural workers in the Pacific an element of danger which has little to do with the natural disasters which menace primitive farming, or with the land and population problems which came in the wave of the white man's hygiene and medicine. The ties which bind the farmer or the peasant of the East to the industrial countries of the West have multiplied with extraordinary rapidity, and only the world depression has slowed their growth. The world depression has been no more disastrous to the farmer and worker of the United States than to the native of Java.

How vitally this relationship has affected the character of the white man's empire in the East has become steadily clearer. The United States looked with national fervor on the Philippine Islands thirty years ago, as a tropical extension of its frontier, a potential source of that agricultural wealth denied to countries farther north of the equator. Today, at congressional hearings on independence for the Philippines, the cotton-seed industry of the South, Utah beet-sugar interests, and the dairy farmers of the Middle West unite to press for independence. A tariff, they believe, to bar competing products from the Philippines, is one of the essential conditions for the restoration of their lost prosperity. This is a far cry from the feelings with which, only a generation ago, we welcomed our "little brown brothers."

This problem does not concern the United States alone. A twenty-year program for the stimulation of rice growing in Korea, begun shortly after the war, has enormously complicated the situation of Japanese rice growers in Japan itself. The expansionist thrust would seem here, too, to have turned back against itself. The world depression, battering down agricultural prices with special severity, has presented problems to the imperial powers of the Pacific which are not easily answered within the terms of "wardenship" over colonies nor within those even of simple self-interest.

These, then, are some of the issues which have grown from the struggle of the industrial, Western nations for control of the land and agriculture of the Pacific. They are for the most part questions which are not resolved in the simple language of the early empire builders. Whether they hinge on the relationship between populations and the land they till, or on the application of labor or capital to the land, or on the new dependence of primitive peoples on distant markets, they break awkwardly through the formulae on which the empires grew.

Even where dry farming and extensive agriculture provide possible areas for resettlement of populations, migration can hardly be expected to provide an all-embracing answer. The empty territory available for large shifts of people in the Pacific at present is definitely limited. In the long run, these problems must be answered in the regions in which they have arisen. For France, Great Britain, Holland, Japan, and the

United States, the imperial powers most concerned in the agricultural problems of this area, they lie at the very base of any continued expansion. Even the preservation of colonial dominions in their present form seems to many to demand new colonial policies.

The more enlightened colonial administrators in the Pacific are struggling to find these answers. In the colonial offices of Western powers earlier policies are being subject to reappraisal. What substitutes can be found which will in some measure work, few would venture to predict.

It seems clear to many that new policies must be directed more effectively to raising the standard of living among native peoples and equipping them more successfully to control their agricultural environment. Either population control or the introduction of new farming methods measurably increasing yields will be essential in many regions if some balance between numbers of people and the food they consume is to be achieved. Some form of capital accumulation, either through credit or by another means, must give these peoples purchasing power if the exchange between them and industrial countries is to continue. In place of land alienation, a method must be worked out for ownership of producing land by those who work on it.

The very statement of these issues suggests the conflict which has arisen and is likely to arise from them. The conflict has in the past occurred between imperial powers in their struggle for unexploited land and resources, or between a Western power and an Eastern people. As the area of unexplored or empty land decreases, the latter conflict seems likely to grow more menacingly in importance than the former. The conflict between the United States and Spain in the Pacific has been succeeded by at least the threat of conflict between American interests and those of Filipinos. Rivalry between modern empires for control of food resources in the Pacific is perhaps not yet at an end. It does not appear at the present time, however, to hold the same dangers of explosion as exist in the relation between these empires and their colonial subjects.

How far the forces which have so far shaped imperial expansion in the Pacific may prove to be capable of answering these problems is an open question. If they do not, the span of this great wave of empire may have reached its end.

MISSIONARIES OF EMPIRE

MISSIONARIES OF EMPIRE
Pearl S. Buck

IN ANY brief review of the part the missionary impulse has played as a movement of history between the West and the East, it is natural to ask how much of the fruit of that impulse will remain in the civilizations where it has sought to express itself. Of the early Christians nothing at all remains in the East except a few historical monuments in scattered spots. Of the later Catholic missions almost as little remains; indeed, it is a question whether these early Catholic fathers did not rather impress upon Europe their own enthusiasms for a high Oriental civilization rather than upon the Orient their own religion. The curious reluctance of still later missionaries to adapt the rites and customs of the form of Christianity to which they were accustomed, their general inability to distinguish between what was the essence of their faith as disclosed by Christ and what was superimposed by history and by association with other civilizations, and at the same time their blind and complacent acceptance of benefits conferred by imperialistic and unjust treaty rights, un-Christian in their very being, must remain forever an astonishment to the impartial and detached mind of any nationality. Therefore, even the most optimistic person, if he is unbiased, cannot say that Christianity has become as yet an integral and indigenous part of any of the Oriental cultures to which the missionary impulse has carried it.

The Christian missionary movement itself, however, has been one of the greatest cultural movements of all time. In it, in the last century and a half, the United States has played the most important part. But it is not possible to understand fully its part without realizing that long before this period Christian missions to the Far East had been going on, and that the Christians in the United States were simply putting the new life of a new country into an old mode.

It is difficult for persons who are not imbued with the spirit of missions to realize how important a cultural drive the missionary impulse has been, for to them it has been a phenomenon to be viewed with amusement or with scorn, with alarm or with resentment. In his own country the missionary has often found little understanding outside of his own groups, and novelists and playwrights have delighted to portray him in his most humorous aspects, ridiculing his seriousness, his sense of divine appointment, his attempts to superimpose his own ideas of morality upon happy and sensuous heathen. In the more civilized countries, such as China and Japan, to which the missionary has gone, he has been met with fairly continuous resentment, sometimes with alarm, and at best only with indifference, except in individual cases. Only among less articulate and less self-aware peoples has the missionary found acceptance, and even there too often child-like wonder and amusement with something new has changed into a ruthless sudden driving out of a foreign element. The story of the missionary impulse and whither the impulse has carried men and women, how it has scattered them over the earth and mingled them through the nations, is a strange one, filled at times with a majesty of heroism unparalleled in any other tale, of death fearlessly accepted, of deprivation beyond human endurance, yet cheerfully endured; and at the same time it is a story often tinged with frailty and pettiness, and at times of actual chicanery.

In this the story of the missionary movement differs in no wise from the story of any other cultural movement in history. Indeed, it is not difficult to understand the missionary impulse at all. It is not a manifestation in any sense unique or fanatic, nor are missionaries any more peculiar than was Columbus or Balboa, or in more recent times, Peary or Byrd. The difference has been in the cause which drove them forth, not in the spirit which moved them. The same spirit has impelled modern scientists, even modern artists. The missionary impulse, therefore, is no strange, ridiculous, alien thing, peculiar to a peculiar individual, or to a peculiar group, or even to a peculiar time in history. Rather, it has been a part of history, a manifestation of the human spirit of the time, whatever the time, and it cannot be understood if it be lifted up out of that place and viewed separately any more than the story of the American Revolution can be understood without its context of time and circumstance. That the Catholic Ricci chose to be a missionary rather than an explorer, that Robert Morrison was a missionary rather than a merchant, that John Nevius was a missionary rather than a diplomat was merely a matter of temperament and chance. All three were expressions of their times, men in whom the ferment of their age worked, and the ferment worked, not because they happened to be Christians, but because they were sensitive and keen men, able to feel the times and to catch the promise. Yet, being Christians, it was natural that they should carry with them as their impelling force not curiosity primarily, nor commercial interest, nor interest in international relations, all of which they might have had, but that they should carry the religious point of view, which was as surely their particular genius as the explorer's urge or the trader's instinct or the diplomatist's flair might be to another.

In other words, the missionary cannot be understood if he is viewed as an anomaly, for he is not an anomaly. He is a product of his environment. Nor can the missionary impulse be understood or rightly valued if it is considered as fanaticism or as a sport in human nature. It must be considered as a manifestation of the general human feeling of an age, working through a person of mystical or religious genius. And it must be borne in mind that this mystical or religious genius is itself a common enough phenomenon, so that it also must be considered a fairly ordinary manifestation. It is a part of every creative worker's mental and spiritual equipment, and lacking the instinct for adventure, it may produce or partly produce the stuff of which poets and painters are made. Added to the instinct for adventure, it has produced the noblest of the missionaries and accounts for the fact that the periods of highest adventure and greatest exploration in human history, adventure either physical or spiritual, and exploration into unknown lands or seas or into human development, are also the periods when the missionary impulse has been most active, and when the missionary type has usually been most vital and most admirable.

One interpolates the word usually, for it must be recognized that oftentimes the missionary impulse was so completely a part of its times and of movements of the day that it did not emerge as individual at all, and was rather only an aspect of military conquest, of exploration, or of commercial extension. It is no accident that the three great periods of missionary zeal in the West coincide with the three periods of expansion in other lines.

The expansion of Christianity between the fifth and sixth centuries into the Germanic world was, for example, in its very nature purely political. The conquerors took their religion with them as part of their imperialism and as an essential part of their culture, to be forced upon the masses of the vanquished as the price of their vanquishment, and for a long time in this period the church was involved with the state and dominated by political influence. Indeed, Christianity had already become so mixed with superstition and formalism that much of its missionary force was gone, and if it was forced upon a vanquished people, the force was mitigated by the fact that the conquered peoples made little fundamental change in belief or ritual, merely substituting the names of the saints and Mary for their own gods.

The Catholic missionaries to the Far East of the sixteenth century in like manner accompanied or preceded explorers not solely, and in some cases perhaps not even partly, out of pure religious zeal, but because they were themselves at heart explorers, religiously inclined, who, either consciously or not, seized upon their religion as an adequate reason for wandering forth into unknown lands. It is interesting to remember that the spirit within the very church itself was not at this time missionary. The whole Reformation was a political rather than a religious movement, and its leaders were striving to purify not so much religion as the legal abuses of priests and popes. In the reformers there was no sense of obligation toward people of other nations. Luther himself was opposed to foreign missions, and his followers later stigmatized plans for a more evangelical religion as "casting the holy things of God before dogs and swine." This attitude, however, undoubtedly had its reflex in driving the Catholic Church to renewed missionary effort, in order to regain territory lost by the Reformation, a purpose which can scarcely be called profoundly religious, although it was doubtless augmented by the fact that it coincided with the period of exploration.

Yet the missionary impulse cannot be understood if it be regarded merely as a movement springing out of a disgruntled Catholic body. The spread of early Christianity into Europe made it an inherent part of

the peoples there, and when in the fifteenth and sixteenth centuries the Ottoman Turks, swarming out
from Asia Minor, threatened to shut off European trade,
religion together with trade was forced to find a new
vent, since this was a period of a great outburst of new
energy in many lines. There had been a thousand years
of struggle and readjustment in Europe, and now there
was an ardent emergence of new life and force in intellectual, emotional, and material desires. Ocean exploration became, therefore, a necessity, and European
culture, of which religion was the vanguard, in the next
four centuries, encircled the globe.

It is interesting to realize, too, that the professed
missionary in this age at least was not the sole expression of the religious impulse. The part religion had in
every explorer was necessarily emphasized. Lonely
ships, sailing unknown seas, manned by a few ignorant
men, were naturally encompassed by great and fearful
dangers, and it was inevitable that in the face of a vast
and unconquered nature these men should cry out the
more to the God they knew and worshiped, and should
feel more acutely their dependence upon the supernatural, or that, having reached in safety some strange
shore, they should with new fervor thank the God in
whom they had trusted upon the seas. Inevitable, also,
that it should be thus with all settlers in new and
foreign lands.

So the history of the missionary movement has been
a curiously peripatetic one, always the vanguard in
the cultural movements of the human race, pushing
on to new fields before it has gathered harvest in a field
already sown. In no country, upon no people, has

Christianity maintained a steady hold. A hundred years before the Reformation the missionary impulse had already cooled, and although Europe by then was nominally Christian, the countries earlier Christian in Asia Minor, in northern Africa, and in Palestine had become Mohammedan. Only in Spain was there any real struggle going on, and here the Christian faith was most alive, so that, when the Spanish and Portuguese explorers went forth, they had as part of their motive the spread of the Christian faith.

And it is curious to behold in the great missionary individuals of the period also this mingling of the religious and the wanderer. Xavier, for example, in the sixteenth century would rest nowhere. In nine years he roamed from Goa on the west coast of Hindustan, to Malaya, and then to Japan. There he wandered afoot for two and a half years, only to return again to Goa, and to be entranced by the thought of China, which, however, he never reached, dying on the little island of Sancian, off the southeast coast. And if there was this intermingling of motive in the individual missionary of the times, it was true of governments as well. England and Holland, Protestant governments, stipulated in trade charters granted to colonial companies that in addition to trade these companies should also spread the Christian religion among the Oriental peoples, and in the earliest colonizing and trading expeditions chaplains were sent together with goods. But it must be acknowledged that mission interests were always secondary to colonial ones, and where there was conflict, colonial interests took precedence, at least until the period of great missionary activity in the seventeenth century.

This formal recognition of the place of religion in Western culture had, of course, insufficient impetus in itself to account for the tremendous growth and expansion of the missionary impulse of the nineteenth century. Heretofore missions had been chiefly Catholic. Now the Protestant churches began to feel the pressure of expansion, and correspondingly the Catholic missions were for a while weakened, although this weakening was perhaps due to one of the most crucial controversies in the history of Christian missions, which occurred at the end of the seventeenth century. This controversy is known as the Rites Controversy, and it is important culturally because it set a Western and even a national stamp upon all of the missions to come. In brief, the controversy centered about the question as to whether or not Christianity should make any compromise with existing rites and religions in the Oriental countries to which it was carried. In the early days of Jesuit missions, when the missionary impulse was not strong in the home church, and when Europe was torn with wars and dissensions, it became increasingly the attitude of the missionaries to adapt Christian rites very markedly to those of native religions. It must not be forgotten that practically without exception every Oriental country resisted most earnestly the efforts of missionaries; in spite of the bright accounts of individuals to the contrary, it has been a fact that from earliest time resistance and not welcome has been the rule. Against the stern persecutions in Japan, against the stubborn denial at first even of entrance

[249]

into China, and then of opposition there, it is not to be wondered at that the Jesuits thought, in the face of the fewness of their numbers and the incredible size of the task undertaken, that it would be justifiable to modify such Christian rites as were most objectionable to Orientals, and to hope that the foreign religion, so modified, might find a place in Oriental culture. Ricci, in particular, was in favor of such modification in China, where he himself admired so profoundly the teachings of Confucius. But incoming Dominican and Franciscan missionaries took the opposite view, and appealing strongly to the Pope, secured his tentative support. Throughout the seventeenth and into the eighteenth century the controversy continued until the bill of 1742, which finally decided the case against the Jesuitical point of view, although not until nearly the end of the century was it completely enforced.

This controversy had several important and lasting effects. In the first place, it showed the lack of unity in the Christian Church, a lack tragically apparent afterwards in Protestant denominations as well, and this weakness has been one of the chief causes of the failure of Christian missions to make Christianity an integral part of the civilizations and peoples to which the missionary impulse has carried it. In the second place, it fixed an attitude of mind in Christians at once intolerant and uncompromising, which has, in its refusal to recognize any value or truth in other religions, made Christianity still foreign in the Orient to this day, and in the past even the awakening of the Renaissance failed to lift this weight of intolerance from the missionary impulse.

But the Renaissance did awaken other tendencies, and again it is interesting to see that missions and the missionary impulse are only an expression of the age. Individualism, revolt against the traditionalism of the Middle Ages, the necessity for expansion, brought into existence the idea of fresh exploration and colonization, and the physical as well as mental liberation of the age, with its new emphasis on the rights of individuals to think and achieve, had inevitable results upon missions. Again the spirit of the times touched minds naturally daring and restless, whose innate quality was at the same time religious, and the beginning of the evangelical movement in England, with its breaking away from the traditional state church, began naturally to follow the spirit of the age, which carried them into every country in the world.

The year 1792, therefore, begins the era of modern missions, as well as the era of Western aggression in the Orient. It is no idle accusation which Orientals make when they associate Christian missions with Western imperialism. It is true that the two are part of the same aggressive movement. The association of Christianity with English government in India, the advantage taken in China by missionaries of every treaty right wrested by conquering wars, the plots among early Christian groups in Japan against the government, the later opening of Japan by force and the apparent lack of any sensitivity on the part of churches and missionaries to the simple ethics involved, give indubitable grounds for the feeling which has steadily persisted in the Orient against the cultural imperialism of missions. The only excuse which can be offered is that missionaries were the fruit of the times which produced them, and it must be remembered that it was the common belief of those times that colored races were not to be considered equal to the white race and that their civilizations were infinitely inferior to those of the West. If colonists and conquerors seized trade and territory and felt no compunctions, it is not perhaps surprising if those whose interest was in religion should express the imperialism of the period in that field as well. Credit must be given the missionary, too, for a genuine belief in the worth of his cause, and for a really unselfish desire to share what he had, and to save, as he thought, childlike and depraved or savage peoples from everlasting torment. In contrast to many traders, the missionary was on the whole a genuine and unselfish person, following his imperialistic motive with courage and conviction of its benefit to those upon whom he imposed it. And it is equally true that there were benefits flowing from the missionary impulse. In the century and a half of the imperialism of the West in the Orient, it would be unjust to deny very real benefit; exactly as there have been decided benefits to India from British government and to the Philippines from American. So missionaries, as a part of the era of imperialism, have conferred cultural advantages upon the people to whom they went.

Opinion must differ as to the measure or the quality of these advantages. But even the most critical and detached mind must recognize that, while missionaries have on the whole not failed to take advantage of rights gained by war or by force, yet, on the other hand, they have also been the first, in later times, to recognize the wrongfulness of using rights so gained, and they have often been foremost in declaring principles of international justice and equality. Within the Oriental countries themselves they have been of great help socially. It is beyond question that to missionaries is due the credit for opening schools and for introducing the idea of opportunity for women, for agitation and education against local customs such as footbinding and opium-smoking, for the introduction of modern medicine. In other words, missionaries brought with them the best elements of their own culture, and these elements were as inevitably a part of their religion as they themselves were of the movement of the times which urged many Europeans and, later, Americans to travel eastward. In England, moreover, the new evangelical period in the Non-Conformist Church was marked by a fresh sympathy for humanity, so that ever since that time missions have been closely linked with philanthropy. This was the more inevitable, since the nineteenth century was the time of great philanthropical beginning. The callousness and polish of the eighteenth century had given way to a rise in the belief of the individual, and the churches merely reflected, sometimes earlier, sometimes later, the spirit of those times.

This new individualism produced an astonishing number of great individual figures in missions. In Japan, Hepburn, Brown, and Verbeck; in China, Morrison, Milne, Guteloff, Bridgman, Williams, and Parker, and others, were all men of brilliant natural gifts, extraordinary character, and unquestioned devotion to idealism, who would have made notable achievements in any land or age. Their understanding of the countries to which they went, their patience and courage, their resolute and statesmanlike planning of the task under-taken, their scholarship both in their own culture and in the Oriental ones, cannot be too highly praised. This was also the period of noble individuals in science and in literature, the period, indeed, of full flowering of European culture, and of first flowering of the stability of the new American nation, rich in its tradition of noble pioneers. The West was never to be more sure of itself than in the nineteenth and beginning of the twentieth centuries, and its missionaries shared in this certainty.

But the period of great individualism and of great missionary individuals began at the beginning of the present century to change. The age of pioneering in the United States was over. The age of mass production and efficiency had begun. In England also the evangeli-cal churches were beginning to consider how Oriental peoples could be more quickly and efficiently "saved." Hudson Taylor is the chief exponent of the new spirit in England, and was chiefly responsible for attracting to China in particular large numbers of persons who, while their motives were doubtless of the best and most kindly, nevertheless were not themselves of the same caliber mentally or spiritually or intellectually as the great pioneers. The same was true in America. Just as later average settlers followed the bold early leaders into the West, so the early missionaries were followed by large numbers of men and women who had been trained in ideas of mass conversion. The slogan of the times was "The world for Christ in this generation."

It was inevitable that the caliber of the individual should be less high than it had been. It was inevitable, too, that there should be less effort made by the missionary, trained in so hasty a school of thought, to become learned in the new civilization to which he went.

In the United States particularly the period was one of large and confident nationalism, the confidence of a favored, rich, and self-satisfied people, charitable because charity was easy. This spirit naturally pervaded the churches, and equally those who went as missionaries from these churches. Consequently, one finds foreign missions at this time carried on in a spirit of arrogance, often unconscious but none the less real, of self-confidence in the uniqueness of the Christian religion, of intolerance of Oriental religions. The bursting enthusiasm of a young and rich country, miraculously and swiftly successful, gave to its missionaries the same easy enthusiasm and belief in its religion as part of the cause for its success. Without meaning to do so, often without knowing that they did, missions propagated Western culture, and especially American culture, as an essential part of the Christian religion. American ideas of government, the American system of education, American types of hospitals were all begun in Japan, Korea, and China. When later Orientals became alarmed and accused missionaries of cultural imperialism it cannot be denied that their accusations were just, although missionaries might and did indignantly deny them, believing honestly that these social services were but means to the great end of the propagation of Christianity.

But the two years of 1914 and 1927 mark the end of

the period of self-confidence. The World War, it is a truism to repeat, shook the sublime faith in itself which the West had had, and missionaries shared in the feeling. It had become an unexpressed but very actual subconscious belief of the missionary that the sinfulness of the heathen accounted to a large extent for his ills. Previously it was preached often, at least by implication, that if the Oriental countries would accept the God of the Christians, undoubtedly that God would give them also the benefits which belonged at the present only to the West. The Orientals had begun to wonder if possibly this might not be true, and they had turned to the study, and even in certain lines the adoption, of Western civilization as never before. Naturally, the Christian religion, as a part of this civilization, was more welcome than it had been, especially as men of learning in the Orient were no longer able, with the incoming of Western science, to believe in much that their own religions taught, so that in China at least there was a decline in the native religions and a real eagerness to hear Christianity.

Then came four years of disillusionment. The wondering Orientals saw a Western world racked by strange punishment and calling upon God, a divided God, since enemies each claimed him and clamored for his aid, and yet none was delivered. Missionaries also were puzzled and confounded and ashamed. Among the more honest, considerable soul-searching took place, and separation began to be made, at least intellectually, between Christianity and Western civilization. The latter was no longer so surely nor so obviously the fruit of the former.

The Oriental was not slow to see the separation and to question the value of a religion which produced no better or more harmonious result among its adherents than the greatest war in history. At least, no Oriental religion would have sanctioned such a catastrophe.

From this hour the disintegration of missions began, because the impulse itself was shaken, the old divine belief gone. The mad years that followed the war, the economic readjustment, the desperate longing for refuge in pleasure, the selfishness of the individual search for such refuge, the lack of idealism in the young, both of those disillusioned in the war and of the generation immediately after, all had their inevitable results upon the missionary movement. The missionaries who went abroad during the years between 1918 and 1927 were for the most part not of the caliber of the period immediately preceding them. To them the work was often in large measure an escape. There were many individuals notably lacking in mental ability and in qualities of leadership and boldness. There was not the enthusiasm and self-confidence of the years of mass production in missions as well as in machines.

When, therefore, in 1927, there came the crisis of certain long-gathering anti-Christian, anti-foreign trends in China, many of the missionaries, particularly the younger ones, could not withstand the blow, and the missionary movement was severely struck. In Japan the blow had already come, though in no such dramatic fashion. With the rapid growth of a new nationalism, extraordinary growth of industrialism, and modern life, there came at the same time a tremendous growth in atheism. Atheistic science converted Japan as the missionaries had never been able to do, and to-day the average Japanese does not consider the Christian missionary as either essential or desirable, although his presence is tolerated on international grounds.

But in China the situation has been far more delicate. The missionary group itself has of late years been divided into two camps, representative of at least two schools of modern thought. The conservatives, naturally less in number in these modern times, have steadfastly refused to accommodate themselves to the growing demands of nationalism and have persisted in maintaining the old ideas of unique religious supremacy for the Christian religion. The liberals fall into two groups, those of more stoutness of heart who have done all they could to adjust themselves and their faith to the changes of the hour, trusting to time to soften the edge of the opposition of agitators, and those perhaps more sensitive and certainly more receding souls, who have felt the opposition intolerable, have questioned the ethics of remaining in countries where they are not wanted, and have finally withdrawn. This division, this doubt and self-distrust, have been characteristic of a world in spiritual as well as material chaos, and no group more faithfully reflects this chaos than does the missionary body.

What might have been accomplished had Ricci and his followers been allowed to work out their ideas of adapting Christian rites to Oriental customs cannot be known. The fact that missions have operated for the most part on a basis of fairly complete intolerance must have been a serious impediment to progress, if not an actual weakness. The history of Buddhism in its spread from India to China and Japan shows that no real hold was gained by it until it had become adjusted to the people to whom it was preached. In China such adjustment took five centuries. It is, of course, obvious that certain native rites and customs, which run contrary not only to Christian principles but to commonly accepted standards of social conduct, could not be tolerated by missionaries. But it is a question whether or not other customs, full of meaning to the people to whom they belonged, and not in themselves anti-social, as, for example, the Confucian ideal of ancestor reverence, might not have properly been adapted by Christians and this with benefit to the West.

Yet nothing could be farther from the truth than to say the missionary impulse has been of no cultural value. If it has not found its perfect expression in Christianity, if it has had to carry with its precious vital load a weight of dead and unimportant matter, yet the impulse itself has been of noble worth, as great worth as any creative genius, of which it is but a manifestation. For the missionary impulse has as its special material the creation of values of the spirit. As a painter with his canvas and his oils, as a musician with his instrument, so the missionary with the human soul. As truly as any other artist, he struggles to transfer the glorious vision in his own mind to some other and explicit medium. If his materials are poor, if his medium is inadequate, it does not mean that his vision is wrong or that his idea is less worthy of expression. It only means that he must try to find more worthy and more adequate means of creation.

Nor is there danger that the missionary impulse will die from the human soul, any more than genius will forever be dead. It will wane, as it has waned, in periods when all fires have smouldered, when humanity has lived at a low level, sometimes for centuries. But when life leaps high again, and fires of brain and body and spirit burn once more, this impulse will take fresh form in new cultural invasions. The most obvious example of this today is, of course, in the communism of Russia, which in China and Japan and India is displacing in fervor the missionary movement, and exhibits the same qualities of conviction, of self-sacrifice, and of intolerance. The sources of the cultural invasions, the missionary movement, of the future are Russia, Italy, and Germany, and it takes no prophet's eye to discern that the invasions will proceed in the same mingled fashion as has the Christian invasion, by force of arms, by force of trade, by force of the driving spirit within.

But if the effect of the Christian missionary movement from the West to the Far East is to be briefly appraised, it may be said that socially the contact has been beneficial, but individually it has been evil. That is, the social gifts the missionary brought, the humanitarian and cultural aspects, have uplifted and enlightened the Oriental peoples. Today, because the missionary taught the need to save the poor and helpless, Orientals are beginning themselves to examine into cause and cure of floods and famines, of disease and ignorance, of banditry and misgovernment. Social welfare is beginning to be considered an essential part of any government's program, and education as the right of all citizens to be given as soon as practically possible in China and India, as it is already in Japan and Korea. Humanity in the Far East has been immeasurably benefited by the contact through the Christian missionary.

But with this enlightenment and enlargement the missionary has also brought his fetters. Upon people who had it not he has fastened a sense of sin, of spiritual obligation, of inferiority before a despotic personal God; in a word, he has brought with him the hard doctrines of the Puritan and of the conception of hopeless original sin. This, it seems to me, is scarcely to be forgiven him except as one must forgive ignorance anywhere without condoning it. The missionary laid upon no one a load heavier than he himself bore.

How much will remain of Christianity in the future of the Far East it is impossible to tell. Too many things are involved. There is in the Orient as in the Occident a genuine spiritual hunger. If Christianity can supply the need for idealism, it may persist. But unless some new vital flame springs out of old ashes, it is not likely to supply this idealism. In the midst of eager, experimental youth the Christian Church continues to proceed in the main with formal and uninspiring creeds and forms, and communism and People's Movements are supplying the idealism. In such cases it can hardly be expected that Christianity can live on into the future as a force in itself, and its main cultural effect must already be over, in the shape it has given to some Oriental educational and social institutions. . . .Yet if new life comes into religion in the West, it may spread again as it has in the past, forever a manifestation of the human spirit. Or it may be that the force is to come from the Orient this time, and that the strength of communism will be the next chief cultural missionary movement in the world. No one can say.

Of the second cultural influence flowing between East and West, the students who have gone from China and Japan to Europe and the United States for education, there is much less to be said, for it began only in this generation; but its effects upon the future must be doubtless far more important. The missionary did assuredly, whether he knew it or not, interest the peoples of the Orient in the culture of the West. Even more did retributive Western armies interest them in the military knowledge of the West. The Opium Wars in China and the reprisals for the Boxer Rebellion, as well as minor reprisals for individual murders of white men, the enforced opening of Japan by the United States in 1854, served to convince the Orient that there was much to learn from the West. Numbers of Japanese went abroad to discover the secret of the strength of the foreigner. In China, missionaries had sent abroad for education a few of their most able young men and women, hoping to establish by this means a corps of native Christian leaders. A few young Chinese of means went independently. After the establishment of the Boxer Indemnity Fund by the United States government, the number of Chinese students to the United States increased enormously and so continued to increase until very recent years, when exchange difficulties on the one hand and the growing influence of Europe in China, because of the influence of the League of Nations, have drawn certain numbers of Chinese to Europe rather than to America.

The result is that today in the Far East there is a large group of Westernized Orientals who are a medium of culture between East and West. In the first generation it is, of course, unavoidable that these Westernized Orientals form a group difficult to be assimilated by either East or West. The years they have spent in foreign countries have caused in them considerable psychological confusion. Western cultures they have found at once better and worse than their own: better materially, so that they have become ashamed of the comparative backwardness and poverty of the masses in their own countries, and worse in the sense that the high moral standards which they had expected, partly as the missionary's unconscious propaganda, have not been necessarily the accompaniment of the material prosperity. In other words, the very countries from which missionaries came have been less Christian than supposed, so that material goods were not necessarily the fruit of righteousness.

This double discovery has led to a renewed nationalism in the Orientals in Western countries, and they have particularly in recent years been zealous in presenting to the West only those aspects of their own culture of which they could be proud. When they have returned to their own countries, however, no longer missionaries to the West, their pride has often sunk into despondence over the conditions they have found among their own people, and there has been consequently a tendency among them to group themselves together in a social unit, having for the most part their own life, separate from the mass of their country-men. They do not venture far from large coastal cities or centers of modernized Chinese life, and as in the Occident they were small centers of Oriental culture, so in the Orient they are centers of Westernism. They live usually in groups together, their social life on the whole within the group, although this may be sub-divided into other smaller cliques, these being depend-ent on the countries where the members were edu-cated. But the entire group forms a bridge between East and West. At one end is the continuing contact with the West through conversance with Western literature and people and in a naturally partly Western point of view. At the other end is the inevitable contact with conditions in their own countries.

In Japan the returned student has been, perhaps, a more successful cultural agent than elsewhere. Driven often by a genuine spirit of patriotism he has devoted himself to sharing with his countrymen the benefits, real or imagined, of his Westernization. It has been this sense of responsibility which more than any other one thing has made Japan into a modern country in so short a time.

In China the effect upon the masses has been less than in Japan, partly because of the size of the masses and partly because fewer of the Westernized group have had a sense of mission for the less favored in their own country. Yet here also a change is coming, chiefly because so large a proportion of the new government are Western-educated Chinese. Through governmental policies and through newspapers, magazines, and books, chiefly, the modern Chinese is beginning to shape his country culturally along the patterns of the West. The most notable and well known cultural effect of the modern Oriental in China has of course been the movement known as the Literary Renaissance, to which must be given the credit for the simplifying of the written language and the consequent burst of new written expression. But it may be fairly just to say that as yet the influence of the modern Oriental in China has been along academic rather than social or scientific lines. Except in one or two instances, the Western-trained Chinese groups tend to associate themselves with university, government, or literary centers, rather than to mingle in the life and problems of ordinary people. This is not true in Japan, where the smallness of the country and the continued existence of a stable government have shortened the period of transition between old and new. In China, the assimilation of the new is still very imperfect and, one feels, must remain so until the young moderns become more native to their countries, as doubtless they will, in another generation.

Yet at the same time an increasingly acute missionary sense toward the West is developing in these modern Orientals. Though secretly intensely critical of their own civilization, inherited national pride is great, so that it has become almost a fetish in many modern Orientals to see that nothing except what is beautiful and good, even if not wholly true, shall be presented to the watching West.

Of these two cultural forces, the missionaries from West to East and the modern Chinese trained in Western culture, it is fairly obvious that the second one will be the more effective in the future. The changing aspect of the missionary impulse, its transference into other causes, the lessening of interest in religion *per se* in the West, the new sensitivity between peoples which doubts the right of one to proselytize another, the enlarging of religious understanding to include more than one religion as true, the loss of belief in the supernatural magic in Christianity, these and many other reasons are enough to cause the change in missions which we see in present times.

But there will be doubtless an increase of cultural education between nations—not only of Orientals studying Western subjects, but of Occidentals turning to the East for serious study in philosophy, literature, history, and art. This later second cultural influence, the interest of the intellectuals in cultures other than their own, will be one of the great unifying forces in the world of the future. Such a growth cannot but be welcomed, for on a basis of this mutuality alone can a sound international understanding be built for the future.

THE OPEN DOOR

THE OPEN DOOR
Tyler Dennett

No realistic statement of the processes by which the West has sought to "civilize" the East could be complete without an appraisal of the part played by the Far Eastern policy of the United States. We have seen the concrete ways in which this policy manifested itself, in many sections of this book. But preliminary to any connected story of how our secretaries of state framed their policies there should be some definitions, and they should be given, as far as may be, in their historical perspective. As far as may be; yes, we should be modest about the possible success of our efforts to reconstruct in imagination the conditions of American national life out of which the foreign policy was born. The first hundred years of contact with the Far East carried the American people very far from the simple beginnings; the last thirty-five years have borne us even farther. Probably we never shall be able to know exactly in what proportion the motives were mixed which sent the American government farther and farther into the politics of eastern Asia. But, first of all, some definitions, the best we can devise.

The corner stone of traditional American policy in the Far East was the demand for unconditional most-favored-nation treatment. Asking no special favors of their own government, the American merchants in the Far East desired only a fair field of competition. They did not wish to be placed under the handicap of having to compete with traders of other nations who could invoke the political intervention of their respective governments to influence the decision of the Oriental customer. This policy was eventually given a limited definition, in the Open Door notes of John Hay, American Secretary of State, in the last year of the last century.

These famous notes sought to secure the voluntary assent of the trading nations, not to a doctrine of free trade in China, but merely to the principle that the trade of China should remain subject to the conditions of free competition for all nations, irrespective of the political changes which then seemed to be impending. The proposal was primarily commercial, being political only in the sense that it was made by one government to others. Underlying the notes was the assumption, patently correct, that the ancient Chinese Empire was unable to be its own doorkeeper. The powers of Europe had already staked out their claims, and even as the notes were being drafted, at least one power—Russia —was mobilizing its military forces to close the door of free competition in a very rich, undefined area which included certainly Manchuria and perhaps all of northern China. The Open Door notes did not ask that Russia or any other Power relinquish whatever political claims had been acquired, but merely that even in case of the actual partition of the empire among the powers, certain specific conditions of free competition should still be assured to the traders of all nations throughout the area of the ancient state.

Thus stated, the doctrine of the Open Door was, in substance, much older than its author or signer. It had a close affinity with the doctrine of the Rights of Man which infused the Declaration of Independence. It had been asserted hundreds of times outside of China in odd corners of the world not alone by the United States but also by England after the latter became the mechanized workshop of the world. The Open Door principle is obviously to the advantage of any state which has something to sell and feels perfectly confident that under free conditions it can deliver its product at the lowest price anywhere in the world. For more than a generation prior to 1899 England had been in that happy position, and, after the recovery from the panic of 1893 in the United States, certain American manufacturers, notably those who made cotton cloth or steel rails, believed that they also had achieved that blessed state, at least in the markets of the Far East.

The political significance of the Open Door notes was that the American government thus came forward to secure the desired objective, not by a system of commercial or political alliances such as were traditional in Europe, but by the voluntary assent of the trading nations—by a new and more inclusive concert of the powers in which the coercive principle would be replaced by free coöperation based solely upon good faith. The famous notes fitted into a new pattern of statecraft which John Hay, under the direction of President McKinley, was just beginning to fashion. We shall return to this aspect of the notes a little later in this chapter.

The second traditional policy of the United States in the Far East, the integrity of China, while closely akin to the Open Door doctrine, was political rather than commercial. While retaining the principle of voluntary coöperation as distinguished from that of political alliances it was directly contrary to the underlying assumption of the notes of 1899 in that it proposed to conserve the territorial integrity of the Chinese Empire rather than to acquiesce in its partition. This new policy was put forward merely as a unilaterial declaration of policy by the American government on July 3, 1900. The importance of the date is that the powers were then in the midst of mobilizing military forces to march to Peking to rescue the beleaguered legations from the Boxers. It was already known that Russia was gathering a very formidable force, and other nations also were suspected. It was feared that the combined military expeditions, once actually on the ground, would fall apart and improve the opportunity to partition the Empire among them. The policy of July 3rd was, in fact, a witness to the futility, already recognized by John Hay, of the Open Door notes. The latter had been accepted with so many reservations and qualifications as to destroy their value as an international compact, much as the similarly famous Kellogg Pact of 1928 was similarly destroyed. The-integrity-of-China doctrine evoked no more dependable international engagement than had the notes of the previous year. John Hay never to the day of his death had in hand any kind of international engagement—not even an exchange of notes—by which the powers bound themselves to respect either the Open Door or the integrity of China. The foregoing assertion may seem astonishing to those who have not closely examined the correspondence and have been taught to believe that in some definite way John Hay secured these principles, but it is the solemn truth. What John Hay did was to hold the powers together until the legations had been relieved and the troops of all the powers, except Russia, had been withdrawn to an extent which greatly diminished the probability of an international war in China to partition the empire among the powers. In short, John Hay's diplomacy in 1900 had the effect of limiting the conflict which matured in 1904, when Japan and Russia, but not Germany, France, England, and, perhaps, the United States, met each other in Manchuria to settle by the arbitrament of arms the very conflict of interests which John Hay had sought to prevent by his famous notes of 1899 and 1900. Lest as a nation we seem vainglorious about a national hero, it should be added that John Hay's task in those two years was rendered much easier by the fact that none of the European powers, save Russia, believed itself yet prepared for the titanic struggle which was impending, which some already foresaw and many feared.

On the other hand, John Hay left to history the legacy of a slogan which served a useful purpose, and in

1922, at the Washington Conference, the doctrines of the Open Door and the integrity of China were reduced to legal formulas and signed as a solemn treaty by all the powers which had declined to bind themselves to John Hay twenty-two years before—all except Russia, which had not been invited to Washington. In the intervening years there had been much lip service to the Hay slogans and some few pledges, but the latter seldom really meant what their words seemed to say.

The third traditional American policy in the Far East is peculiar to neither the United States nor the Orient. It is the protection of national interests. Every state has such a policy, but no one can ever for very long be sure what it means or implies. There is no dictionary which defines a "national interest"; no yardstick by which to determine whether the interest is actually national or merely local or institutional. Nor does one ever know what may in any unnamed set of circumstances be involved in its protection. American interests in the Far East may be defined in either of two ways. They are the interests of such Americans as live there or have invested their money there—that is the limited definition, and its further meaning may easily be defined by reference to certain census reports and tables of financial statistics. The other definition is latitudinarian: any interest which the national government may from time to time be induced to take up and support by some form of intervention. Such interests become national not by reason of their extent but rather by virtue of the fact that the national government extends to them its protecting arm.

Starting with the restricted definition, one may state that the American interests in China are the nearly seven thousand Americans who live there and the two hundred and forty millions of dollars which we have seen to have been invested there by them or other Americans. These interests are further defined by treaties with China, by some not very clearly defined rules of international law, and by some rather flexible habitudes of the American Department of State. The latitudinarian definition of American interests in China includes all of the foregoing and as much more as any private or semi-public American interest can by political influence or propaganda crowd under the covers at any particular moment. Hence it appears that this third American policy in the Far East really included both of the others, so that the latter are really to be regarded as methods, expedients, which the American government has, from time to time, put forward to achieve the former. We may, however, profitably follow a little further our inquiry as to the nature of American interests in the Far East, for we ought to ascertain, if possible, what have been the motives which have been the pulsating, fluctuating force behind the policy.

If it is difficult to define an American interest, it is even more baffling to define the American mind and soul, and for similar reasons: America is plural even though it requires a singular verb.

This question of motives is the more important by reason of what appears to have been the startling reversal of American policy. For a century the American people, secure in the broad moat which separated them from Europe, and very contemptuous of what seemed to them the antiquated and effete political systems of the other continent, had cherished the simple doctrine of the Two Spheres: the United States would stick to the Western Hemisphere; let the Old World stay at home and mind its own business. From this homely doctrine there had been occasional departures. A notable one had been the Clayton-Bulwer Treaty, which recognized the proposed trans-isthmian canal as a matter of not exclusively American concern, although the intent was to give England another push into the ocean. The Perry expedition to Japan was equally notable, although the American statesmen had never defined the doctrine of the Two Spheres as excluding the United States from a direct interest in the Orient. In the one instance the American government acknowledged the rights of the Old World in the New; in the other instance the United States reached out an arm halfway round the world to exert a powerful, even menacing, interest in the most remote portion of the older sphere. Both of these instances occurred in the mysterious decade of Manifest Destiny which followed the victorious war with Mexico. It does not help much to explain that fifty years later that doctrine of Manifest Destiny again rolled up to engulf the doctrine of the Two Spheres, for that still leaves unexplained the cause in the one instance as well as in the other.

Among the motives which led to the adoption of an aggressive Far Eastern policy in the McKinley and Roosevelt administrations, some were unquestionably philanthropic.

THE OPEN DOOR

The American people, in the midst of the prosperity which followed the lean panic years, were in a crusading mood. The success in Mexico in 1848 had given an impulse to philanthropy in the United States; if one objects to the word, then let us repeat "crusading spirit": the abolition movement, temperance, Protestant foreign missions. Something very similar occurred in 1898 after the war with Spain. To many earnest, peace-loving Americans it seemed a supremely virtuous act to have defeated a decadent, corrupt, and treacherous—so Spain seemed to us then—Old World state and to have expelled it from the Western Hemisphere. Over portions of two continents Spain had too long extended its blighting influence: that was the way we felt about it. By chance, so it seemed, the opportunity to serve benighted peoples was extended to include the Philippines: a heaven-sent opportunity. Of course Cuba must be free; of course the poor Filipinos must be freed from their oppressors and guided out into the blessed path which leads to political righteousness, to republican institutions.

This impulse in 1898 was vigorously nourished by the American Protestant churches.

> *"Wherever man oppresses man*
> *Beneath Thy liberal sun,*
> *O Lord be there, Thine arm laid bare,*
> *Thy righteous will be done."*

Thus had written the man whom President McKinley selected to be Secretary of State. And the churches were not very slow to pick up the verse, and others equally emotional, to include in their hymnals.

How this missionary zeal, political to establish republican governments, and evangelical to preach the Word to every creature in this generation, powerfully supported not merely the retention of the Philippines but, likewise, the whole Far Eastern policy of the United States is discussed in detail elsewhere.

In one other respect the impulse was altruistic and inspired by a sense of responsibility for the condition of the world. In our day it has become common to speak with a sneer of the "White Man's Burden." Both John Hay and William McKinley appear to have had a simple faith in the sincerity of British burden-bearing. The Pax Britannica seemed to them a beneficent condition which was being threatened by the growing dissonance in the Concert of Europe. England had gotten herself into a tight place where the burden of maintaining world peace would have to be either shared or dropped. John Hay came back from London in 1898 ready to guide his country into a "partnership of beneficence," as he described it, with England. Together the two English-speaking nations would stand, not for plunder, nor for any ignoble purpose, as Hay viewed it, but rather to carry forward the great civilizing work which England had begun.

In President McKinley, John Hay found a tolerant though somewhat timid colleague. The President believed in combinations. By such measures he had won his own political way; by such expedients he hoped to see the railways of the United States merge, the telephones combine, the steel companies unite, to eliminate the wasteful, hate-gendering competition. Why should not the same method operate also in the field of international politics? Let the United States join with England in the partnership of beneficence and keep open the articles of partnership until all the other powers could be induced to join the happy, voluntary association. Henry Adams, in his autobiography, described the policy and named it "McKinleyism"; the present writer is merely amplifying the Adams definition.

The spirit of McKinleyism was very similar to that of the later Fourteen Points and the spirit of the still more recent Kellogg Pact. It chorded with an American trait which can be traced in and out through all American political history. It was the pattern into which the Open Door notes of 1899 fitted. This explains in large measure why the famous notes lifted John Hay to such a pinnacle of popularity. The Hay policy had about it a Jim Bludso flavor of quiet chivalry. The retention of the Philippines, the Open Door notes, and the doctrine of the integrity of China a few months later, marked the entry of the United States into the partnership of beneficence which had for its ultimate political object the winning of Germany from gun power to coal power, from military to industrial development; the wooing of France from Russia, and then the encirclement of the latter if the Russian autocracy did not in due time see the light in the new era of peace.

In thus setting forth, without critical comment, this halcyon doctrine of the perfectibility of international relations, we do not wish to mislead: there was another side to the picture. The entry of the United States into world politics through the back door of Asia was not exclusively philanthropic. For example, the partnership of beneficence was initiated by a modest distribution of British assets. The British navy retired in favor of paramount American influence in the Caribbean. This withdrawal, important as it seemed to American statecraft, was actually a compromise with American desire. The political platforms of the major political parties, both in 1896 and in 1900, set up either open or thinly veiled hints at the annexation of Canada.

In some respects the Far Eastern policy of John Hay was a Caribbean policy. In return for the British surrender in the Caribbean, Hay was able to offer no material concessions elsewhere as, for example, along the boundary of Southeastern Alaska. The Americans wanted the whole hog; they would yield nothing. On the other hand, under the guise of getting still more, Hay could greatly flatter the pride of the eagle and, by the same stroke, render England a promising service in Asia. He could send out the Open Door notes at a moment when British trade was being gravely menaced in China, and England was being drawn into a devastating conflict with the Boers and unable to fight for her markets in the Far East. These notes were, in fact, first suggested and outlined by an Englishman, Alfred E. Hippesley, formerly of Sir Robert Hart's staff in the Chinese Maritime Customs. The promise of the first notes was amplified in the second set about the integrity of China. The partnership of beneficence involved in the Far East not so much a distribution of assets as of responsibilities. England got out of the Caribbean, in a sense, and the United States got into the Far East. Perhaps the trade was a good one, but, as we now view it, the price paid by the United States was certainly commensurate with the advantages gained.

There was still another motive lurking in the background and not wearing even the disguise of philanthropy. As already pointed out, the American industrialist was even then demanding new markets. There were two ways to provide them, although in those days the producers recognized only one. Markets to correspond in size to the expanding volume of American manufactures could have been obtained by increasing at home the distribution of profits to the workers, who were the most immediate buyers, or by exporting the surplus produce to other parts of the world and keeping wages down at home to as low a level as possible. The latter alternative was the one which England had followed with so much apparent success; it was the one adopted by the Americans. The opening of Asia to exploitation was an alluring prospect to American capitalists. How important this commercial motive was in the shaping of American policy at the turn of the century it is difficult to say. Some students think that it was controlling. I doubt it, for it assumes on the part of American business a far greater prescience than the record reveals. Nevertheless, there is trustworthy evidence to prove that once the policy had been adopted the American government made definite efforts to sell the idea to its people. The salesmanship was feeble enough compared with that adopted twenty years later when Herbert Hoover became Secretary of Commerce, but those were the days of little things. In 1900 both governments and private agencies had yet to learn what can be accomplished by propaganda.

It is not essential to the development of our line of thought to deal minutely with the various stages through which American policy in the Far East passed until it emerged as a world-wide policy. On the other hand, a rapid summary of some of the major steps will be helpful.

Having adopted a great-power policy in the Far East, the American government was required to increase the scope of its foreign policy in every direction. Having a "Pacific work," as Hay called it, to do, naval bases in the Pacific and a canal at the Isthmus became urgent necessities. On the one hand, it was argued that the canal was essential to national defense, since it would permit the rapid concentration of the fleets in either the Eastern or Western waters. On the other hand, the economy argument appeared. With the canal, it would be unnecessary to have such a large naval establishment because of the proposed means of rapid concentration. But this argument was quickly forgotten, and the canal, once built, far from becoming a measure of military economy, was seen to be a reason for additional naval expansion, since the canal would have to be defended. Construction of a great-power navy to support a great-power policy went forward rapidly under Roosevelt. The American people long have been accustomed to the fact that both naval estimates and navy war plans are based upon the contingency that the United States may at any time be called upon to intervene in the Far East, either to defend the Philippines or to "protect American interests" in China.

The European powers were quick to see that the

United States had, in principle, abandoned the doctrine of the Two Spheres when it entered the Far East. At once they began to set their nets to enmesh the Americans also in the affairs of Europe. Under Roosevelt little urging was required. The Russo-Japanese War, fought in the Far East but fundamentally a European conflict, provided Roosevelt with his first opportunity to intervene. From Portsmouth to Algeciras was but another short step. Under Taft the United States pulled back toward the traditional policy of independent, non-coercive action, but the current was too strong; the next President led the American people to Europe to participate in the war which John Hay and Theodore Roosevelt had envisaged and sought to prevent. In 1919 at Paris, Woodrow Wilson wielded the bolts like Jove himself, to dispose of European boundary lines and European political systems to an extent which would have appeared incredible to almost every American who died before 1905.

The principle of the Open Door Doctrine appeared in the Fourteen Points: "the removal, so far as possible, of all economic barriers and the establishment of an equality of trade conditions among all nations consenting to the peace and associating themselves for its maintenance." Point Three, however, associated with the Open Door principle another—the maintenance of an equality of trade conditions by an association of nations in which the coercive principle would be employed. In this important respect it parted company with the principle of McKinleyism. With this slogan Wilson went to Paris. But in the Covenant of the League of Nations which emerged from the Peace

[283]

Conference, although the coercive principle remained, the principle of the Open Door had disappeared. As for the integrity of China, when the Japanese were in possession of Shantung, Manchuria, and far advanced into Siberia, the Peace Conference, Wilson assenting, evaded the question. The Americans went to Paris with a new Open Door principle; they returned with a shell from which the meat had been removed. President Wilson had participated in the creation of another gun-power concert of Europe to which the Western Hemisphere and eastern Asia were appendant.

Declining to join the new concert, the American government of 1921 called a conference of the powers interested in the Pacific and put through the famous Washington treaties. The principle underlying them was McKinleyism: voluntary association to eliminate cutthroat military competition, another partnership in beneficence. Six years later an American secretary of state advanced McKinleyism a step further by inducing the powers to sign the Multilateral Pact for the Renunciation of War. This was McKinleyism pure and simple: no sanctions, merely promises and the pledged faith of nations. John Hay, had he been alive, could have told them that it would not work. He had been unable to hold the Powers together on a voluntary basis even to maintain the integrity of China and the Open Door. And as for the American people, he could have told them that they would not support in the Far East, at least, a policy any more vigorous. In the latter part of 1900 he had been unable to secure the retention in China of the modest contingent of 5,000 troops which the United States had contributed to the relief of the legations and which Hay and W. W. Rockhill had hoped to employ later to oppose the advance of Russia in Manchuria.

The Kellogg Pact was not enough. It would have been perfect in a perfect world, but in the wicked world in which we live its strength was its weakness. It had no sanctions. The next step was the non-recognition doctrine of President Hoover and Secretary Stimson. Although designed for application anywhere, it was brought forward for the express purpose of preserving the Hay principle of the integrity of China. It had the guise of a non-coercive policy, but actually it was a form of sanction. It is very doubtful whether the American people will sustain it. The flavor of the non-recognition doctrine is more like that of Article XVI of the Covenant than like the Hay notes of 1899 and 1900.

From 1899 to 1933 American policy in the Far East has been one of fits and starts. Starting with McKinleyism it advanced to Rooseveltism, retired to Taftism, advanced to Wilsonism, retired to Hughesism and Kelloggism, and then advanced again to Stimsonism. The principle of voluntary association, the partnership of beneficence, seemed always to require implementation. A policy of peace always turned out to be a policy of intervention. Meanwhile it would appear that, notwithstanding the contrary import of American participation in the World War, the Americans remain a noninterventionist people. They have the mind of a Will Rogers.

In conclusion, let us reëxamine the Far Eastern policy of the United States in the light of its history now extended to more than a third of a century. The policy originally rested and continues to rest upon the dual basis of national interest and philanthropic duty.

The American government expected to get some material benefits out of the partnership of beneficence: it demanded the paramount position in the Caribbean; indeed, in the Western Hemisphere. This was obtained and is now held securely. From no quarter of the globe is it seriously threatened.

The United States also expected to safeguard in eastern Asia the opportunity for unhampered competition in potential markets, the need for which was assumed to be urgent. The assumptions underlying this expectation were two. On the one hand, it was assumed that the path to greater and greater prosperity lies along the way of ever increasing exports. In recent years we have come to call this assumption neo-mercantilism. The other assumption was that, if politics in the Far East continued in what seemed to be their natural course, the doors to American trade would become more and more restricted. It was expected that the possessing nations, the beneficiaries of a partition of the Chinese Empire, would close the door, leaving the American trader on the outside. Few then realized the implicit economic fallacy. Hobson's *Imperialism* appeared in 1901, but Norman Angell's *The Great Illusion* was not published until 1908. We now know that England's best markets were not in Asia, where it thought it required an Open Door, but behind the tariff walls of Europe. And so has it been with the course of American trade. The markets of the Far East have grown, yes, but it cannot be shown that they have grown by reason of the

Open Door. They have increased everywhere with rising standards of living and the perfection of communications. The markets seem to be best where the standards of living are highest, regardless of the flag which waves over the people who buy. Slowly also we have come to appreciate the simple truism that we can sell only in proportion as we buy. The Open Door does not seem to have much to do with the total export trade. The break-up of China, or the closing of commercial doors, does not mean the destruction of either the needs or the produce of four hundred millions of people. The people remain as they were; their government is not likely to be worse than now; it may be improved. And with the improvement there is certain to come an increase of material wants in the supplying of which, directly or indirectly, every trading nation will share.

It therefore remains for the American people to decide whether the material profit from the military expenditure necessary to maintain the Open Door and the integrity of China will ever offset the outlay. As for the protection of "national interests," it is within the control of American taxpayers to give the narrow, not the latitudinarian, definition. It is difficult to see why we should be more alarmed about the markets in Eastern Asia than in Africa, or Europe.

That the American people are turning toward a restricted definition of American "interests" in the Far East is apparent both from the popular acclaim over the Washington treaties of 1922 and the recent action of Congress on the independence of the Philippines.

Now, as to the philanthropic side of traditional Far Eastern policy. This philanthropy, as we have seen, had two phases. On the one hand, there was an evangelical zeal to convert the pagan world to Christianity; to lead them also toward republican institutions. On the other hand, there was the recognition by the American government of a duty to lend its assistance in the maintenance of the peace of the world.

The theory of Christian missions is now in process of restatement. The discussion bristles with controversy into which it is not necessary here to enter. In two respects, however, there is an approach to general agreement.

The missionaries have come to see the ethical absurdity of gunboat support for Christian propaganda. They no longer demand the political intervention of their governments to secure for them the political freedom in which to propagate their doctrines. The alliance of Church and State in the mission fields is now discredited. In 1903, the Republican administration at Washington, zealously playing every possible card to make sure of continuance in power in November, 1904, did not fail to give the missionaries its energetic support. There went into the new commercial treaty with China an amplified form of the religious-liberty clause of the earlier treaty, and new provision was made to ensure most-favored-missionary-treatment as to the purchase of property and the rights of residents in the interior. The extraterritorial privileges of the earlier treaty were, of course, continued. In that same year the President and the State Department were also very zealous in the protection of missionaries by diplomatic intervention and also by displays of naval force, although the latter were more especially directed to the

Near East. The political result was as designed; Roosevelt won a strong following among the missionaries and, what was more important in November, 1904, among the church voters at home who supported the missionaries abroad. Today, certainly very many American missionaries would scorn to be made use of to serve a political purpose as they were used in 1903–04.

The time is rapidly approaching, if not already here, when missionary leaders will recognize that a religious-liberty clause has no legitimate place in a commercial treaty. It is, in fact, an infringement of what should be the sovereign right of every state to regulate such matters by domestic legislation. Already a large number of missionaries have declared that they desire to be freed from the special protection of extraterritorial courts in China, and that they desire to take their chances along with their converts in the national courts. It is safe to say that the opinion is rapidly passing that the propagation of Christianity requires the political intervention of governments. One reason, therefore, which led the Protestant missionaries thirty years ago to support a vigorous Far Eastern policy has disappeared.

The missionary leaders seem also in large measure to have agreed that the rise of nationalism in the Far East must very materially alter in the future the position of the missionary in relation to converts. Hitherto he has been, generally speaking, the master as well as the almoner. Converts are becoming more and more restive under such a relationship. In the future it may be expected that the foreign missionary in China will occupy in the Chinese churches a position more like that of the foreign adviser whom the Chinese government not infrequently employs to give expert advice, but whom it never fails to regard as employee rather than as master. The changing position of the missionary in the midst of rising Chinese nationalism is likely to alter materially the dependence of the former on his own government. An interventionist policy on the part of the United States will unquestionably place the American missionary under an ever increasing handicap.

Now, as to the establishment of republican institutions. Opinion on this point is also changing. President Wilson led the American people into Europe on a consent-of-the-governed slogan. In a large measure we have been disillusioned. Certainly it is no part of American moral obligation to impose on any people a form of government which they do not desire or cannot maintain. To the doctrine of self-determination there are many severe limitations which the American people did not in 1918 adequately comprehend. Christianity, at least Protestant Christianity, is instinct with the genius of republican institutions. Planted in the midst of autocracy, or patriarchy, it is disruptive of existing political as well as social organizations. Its propagation is, at best, the spreading of subversive doctrine; at worst, it amounts to interference in the domestic affairs of another state. Whether the world is, in fact, moving on with halting steps toward the goal of political liberty which all Americans thought they foresaw thirty years ago, is too broad a subject to be debated here. It must, however, be reasonably clear that Christian propaganda abroad can no longer safely bid for support on the ground that it tends to stimulate the growth of republican government.

Thirty years ago the political stability of the Far East was recognized as a very important factor in the peace pattern of the world. It was feared in 1898 that a scramble of the powers in China would rapidly spread back into Europe, where it would precipitate a European war. It did not eventuate exactly that way. Quite possibly, if Theodore Roosevelt had not intervened in 1904 and 1905, the commotion in Manchuria would have communicated to Europe, but this is speculation. At any rate, when the expected war came it started, not in the Far East, but on the edge of the Balkans.

The question now arises whether there is in the Far East any imminent disorder which is likely, as was expected a generation ago, to disturb the peace of the world. On the far horizon, perhaps, are two war clouds. China may, on some dim distant day, rise in its might to expel Japan from the mainland of Asia as Europe once expelled England from the Continent. Certainly the prospect is not one to give any immediate alarm, nor is there any necessary reason to assume that such a conflict, if it were to come in our own generation, need engulf the world as the murder in Sarajevo did. It is possible that on some distant date Russia may go back to Manchuria to play with Japan a return game for the stake it has lost. Theodore Roosevelt, after the Peace of Portsmouth, so prophesied. Opinions widely differ as to whether such a spectacular tournament is imminent.

At present Soviet Russia is, probably, the most pacific power in Europe. It is conserving strength for internal development; it will be a long, long time before the Soviet Union can afford to provoke any military expeditions which will leave its western frontier weakened to even a slight extent. The Soviet face is set toward the West. There it is likely to be fully occupied.

It may be admitted readily that Japan, in contrast, has recently been and may still be in a provocative mood. How long a nation can sustain an emotional condition such as has characterized the last two and one half years is problematical. We do know, however, that such conditions cannot last indefinitely, and the reaction is likely to be swift. That the party now in control in Tokyo may wish to provoke a new situation in Siberia to bolster up a waning popular enthusiasm seems plausible enough. Whether such an effort could succeed is not so certain. Japan already has the object of its heart's desire, the wellspring of patriotic aspirations for forty years.

Even if Japan were soon to start a war with Russia, or even to be drawn into a conflict in Mongolia, it is far from inevitable that the Western powers would be drawn in. They were not so involved thirty years ago in the first Russo-Japanese War. Then, obviously, the powers were not ready for war. Today they have more men either under arms or available, but there is grave doubt as to how many of their sadly disillusioned soldiers would fight their comrades of labor on the other side of any battle line which the political expediency of the moment might lead European statesmen to draw. Nor do the statesmen know where to draw the line. Politically, Europe is less prepared for war in the Far East than in 1904. While admitting the possibility of more war in the Far East, this writer is not disposed to expect it, still less to see it convulse the world.

There remains the larger questions: the so-called peace machinery. Out of McKinleyism, which was really not much more than an American edition of Joseph Chamberlainism, there grew, by accretion and otherwise, the League of Nations, its covenant, the Kellogg-Briand Pact, the non-recognition doctrine. By some it has been felt that there is much at stake in maintaining, even developing these mechanisms. To many it seems that this network of peace structures, spread over the face of the earth, is the finest flower of civilization; that any injury to it is a matter of so great international concern that it should be met with prompt and adequate punishment. Specifically, this thesis called for a very vigorous policy in eastern Asia when Japan set upon China in 1931. It was, indeed, disillusioning to see how easily and with what impunity Japan could break this net and its own plighted word. Perhaps we should be not resentful, but grateful to Japan for having thus disclosed the weakness of our supposed security. At any rate, we now know that the powers cannot be thus easily lured into energetic measures which have for their purpose the mere avenging of broken faith. To arouse the nations there must be involved some material interest such as simply does not exist for them in eastern Asia.

McKinleyism, in which the Open Door and the integrity of China doctrines were the initial chapters, contemplated a political world of harmonious states held together by enlightened self-interest in some such way as competing railways might find it to their advantage to make rate and traffic agreements. The idea was sensible enough, but it could not be realized. In such a world the Open Door principle would have been a principle of cohesion. In the world as we find it thirty years later the Open Door doctrine and the other principles which were found necessary to bolster up its essential weakness are seen to be not principles of cohesion but of division. They are in practice policies of intervention, essential neither to prosperity nor to peace. The Open Door doctrine fits into the pattern of internationalism. The nations, on the contrary, have with one accord determined to return to their ancient nationalistic ways.

Where nations seek to wrest from each other special privileges, whether economic or strategic—and who can doubt that such is the world we live in?—the Open Door principle very quickly loses its apparent pacific character and becomes in fact a policy of intervention. Joined not to internationalism, which is rejected by all the major powers, but to nationalism, which the world and especially the American people have adopted, the Open Door principle is likely to turn out to be little more than the old imperialism with a new name.

PEACE OR WAR

PEACE OR WAR
Nathaniel Peffer

THE note that runs through these chapters is one of conflict: political, economic, cultural, and, substantively or potentially, military conflict—in a word, war. The Far East involves the relations of nations; therefore the first and major question it puts is, Peace or war? There are other questions intrinsically of larger content and deeper import. But, as the affairs of men run in the nationalistic, competitive twentieth century, the resultant question must be, Peace or war? All other questions are dependent on the prior settlement of that one.

Two cultures have met, of disparate development and irreconcilable content, their elements resistant to fusion, if not mutually repellent. The East has been drawn into the Western system. For years it has been a commonplace of political writing that the future was to the Pacific. Shorn of its orotund solemnity and the exaggerated emphasis lent by the expert mind, the platitude has a measure of truth. The truth lies in the deduction to be drawn from the physical fact of the shrinking of the earth as a consequence of faster and easier communications. Two systems have met, because one was able to thrust itself on the other.

We have been dealing, then, in this book not only with a contrast of cultures but a conflict of cultures. Without grasping the full extent of this conflict it is not possible to understand the Far East or the relation of Europe and America with the Far East, in the past, now, or in the future. This is more than a matter of intellectual speculation on the nature of comparative culture, however. For out of the differentiation of a mechanized society and the culture which it informs with its power and spirit from an unmechanized society and the culture from which it is organically inseparable have arisen all those strains which manifest themselves in trade rivalries, struggles for territorial and financial concessions, seizures of territory, shelling of Eastern ports by Western gunboats, and all the preludes and actualities of war, the seizure of Manchuria being the latest. The abstract question takes the most acutely concrete forms in day-to-day political and economic relations.

The discoveries of science and their application to production came first in the West. They were the instruments by which was reared the material structure of industrialism, later buttressed by nationalistic governments and carried to majestic heights by unbridled private enterprise. Thus came about the deviation by the West from the parallel lines of development followed by all races on earth until the end of the eighteenth century. This constitutes the disparity, the contrast of culture, on which so much overblown rhetoric and specious metaphysics have been expended. This was the contrast that made for conflict, that entailed conflict. For by reason of the deviation not only had communications been made easier, but a preponderance of power had been created, a preponderance out of all precedent in previous human history. One system was able to thrust itself on the other, not only because it had been brought nearer, but because it acquired force to put behind the thrust. The discoveries of science made possible power machinery and also high-power artillery.

The point has been made several times in the preceding chapters that we have cherished vain expectations from the Far East. In truth, our trade has not been very large; our investments have not been very large or very profitable; of raw materials we have obtained only a small quantity, since they existed only in small quantity. The argument that may be drawn from these facts, the argument best formulated by Norman Angell in *The Great Illusion,* is that war and the rivalries that culminate in war do not pay, not even for the victorious. We have driven ourselves in aggressions on the Far East which have brought us to the verge of war and sometimes over. The event has demonstrated that the prizes were not worth the risks.

All this is incontrovertible and also irrelevant for practical purposes. It is undeniable that trade and investments have not yielded as much as we thought they would, but the point is that we thought they would and acted as if they would. In practical affairs it matters little if the beliefs that men hold are not founded on the truth so long as they act as if the beliefs were so founded. The forces set in motion by their acts are no less powerful and the results no less positive. Our expectations from the conquest of the Chinese Empire were illusory; but we conquered, which is what matters. And the results in international relations today are no less menacing.

The argument is unreal in another respect. In national economy, as in national politics, there is a tendency to think in abstractions which are fictive, as when we talk of "France" and "England" and "Germany," as if there were such constant entities apart from the millions of individuals who are born in the territories so named.

When we say that the returns from national aggressions and the rivalries that culminate in war do not pay, whom do we imply as the object of the verb to pay? The whole nation, the national economic whole, the aggregate of the individuals who constitute the nation? Then certainly the argument is unanswerable. The mass of individuals certainly does not gain. That is self-evident. It must be remembered that at the end of the nineteenth century, when England's navy swept the seas and the sun never set on the British Empire, in English cities were the worst slums in the world. From the point of view of the national economy, when the cost of armaments and of war is balanced against the returns from that which was won or saved by war, then certainly there is a deficit. That, too, is self-evident. But this is artificial accounting. It is the equivalent of "the economic man" in old-fashioned economics. There is no national economic whole. The fluid aggregate which goes by that name must be separated into its constituent elements before the motive forces that drive nations can be understood. Then it becomes obvious that there are elements which definitely do profit by the gains of war. In other words, the losses of war are paid by everybody, either in actual losses by destruction or in the form of taxation; the gains fall only to some. As it happens, not by accident, those to whom the gains fall are those who have power of decision in the affairs of nations. They do not will wars, of course; they only dictate actions that inevitably produce conflict with other nations in which analogous elements dictate similar actions.

It is not enough to say, then, that "American" trade or "British" trade or "French" trade in the Far East has not been large or profitable. It has not been, indeed, in proportion to the total of trade and investments on the books of those countries. National policies based on the expectations of large profits from exploiting the Far East have been mistaken, indeed, from the point of view of the advantage of all the British, American, or French people—or Japanese people, for that matter. But there have been groups in England, France, and the United States which most decidedly have profited from the Far Eastern trade, and profited enormously. And those are the groups which have had the ruling voice in determining British, French, and American policies. To apply the argument to current events, even if the strains caused by the Japanese adventure in Manchuria should tear the economic fabric of Japan, to say nothing of crushing the Japanese peasants and artisans with taxes, there are large groups in Japan which will come off better, nevertheless. It is they who support, if they have not helped initiate, the Manchurian adventure.

The expectations from the Far East may have been illusory, then; but that is irrelevant so far as the development of Far Eastern international relations is concerned. Whether or not Occidental penetration in the Far East has been profitable, and regardless of whom it profited, the fact is that we acquired the power to penetrate and that we did so. In result, all of Eastern Asia from the Indian frontier to the islands off the continental coast fell into substantive possession or effective control by one or more of the great powers, Japan alone managing to retain independence. It was China, however, that bore the full weight of the thrust. China was and is the most coveted prize in the Far East. Its size, riches, and potential energy make it the greatest stake of empire. By virtue of its size, riches, and potential energy, also, it is the focal point, the gravitational center, of the Far East. In China the great powers broke down the barriers to European trade. They occupied the principal ports. They seized territory and stationed troops at strategic points. They acquired the right to fix China's tariff on imports and thereby gained control of its fiscal policies and financial sovereignty. They exacted the privilege of extra-territoriality, thus obtaining immunity from Chinese legal jurisdiction and taxation. They marked out regions of China as their respective spheres of influence; had not the exigencies of European political complications intervened, China would have been formally partitioned. Only now Japan has appropriated to itself by forcible seizure the Manchurian provinces and large parts of Mongolia.

This process has not been bilateral only. It has not lain between one constant entity, the aggressor, and another, the victim. There have not been only two parties to the conflict—China on the one side, the powers on the other. There has been conflict between China and the aggressors, and conflict also between shifting groups among the powers. In China was reflected the mounting rivalry of the European powers, the intensifying struggle that worked to climax in 1914. In fact, the rivalry was to a great extent laid in China since it was essentially a rivalry for the perquisites of empire, for the privileges and profits of exploitation of the undeveloped parts of the earth, undeveloped by the standards of industrialized society. While all the great states of the world brought their military might and diplomatic skill to bear on the increasingly helpless Manchu court at Peking, they also directed the same resources to thwarting each other in the Far East. The Battle of the Concessions in the 1890s was waged against China by the principal European powers and, also, by one power against another. Russia took Port Arthur; England countered with Weihaiwei as a naval base. The first major war directly caused by lust for the spoils of the Far East was fought between Russia and Japan. Then the Far East was overshadowed by the outbreak of the main struggle in Europe. Before the aftermath of the World War had settled, the Far East emerged into prominence again, Japan now forcing the pace of aggression. The Washington Conference was held in 1921, but it brought only the semblance of truce.

A complicating factor was introduced by the advent of nationalism in China and its feverish growth. China turned on the aggressors, which were forced to protect their possessions and privileges as far as they could. Only Soviet Russia and Japan were in a position to do so. The former frustrated China's effort to recover the Chinese Eastern Railway in northern Manchuria in 1929. Japan took the offensive as the best defense and settled the smouldering controversy over southern Manchuria by invading and seizing it and then, adding northern Manchuria thereto, creating the pretense of an independent state in Manchoukuo. Today the international process as of before 1914 has been resumed. Russia and Japan confront each other again, much as they did in 1902. Japan has trenched on Russia's rights and possessions in northern Manchuria, emboldened by Soviet Russia's manifest desire to expend its energies on the consolidation of the revolution within its own borders. At the moment of writing Soviet Russia has given notice: so far and no further. At least as important, the United States and Japan are arrayed against each other over Manchuria. The United States refuses to recognize the separation of Manchuria from China; meanwhile Japan rules Manchuria.

On all historical precedent it may be said conclusively that this is a situation that cannot long be held in suspense. The Far East has been drawn into the Western system, a dependent part of which is the system of nationalistic wars for economic exploitation. It cannot long remain a theater of war without the enactment of the drama proper to itself. All the forces of conflict latent in the Far East for a hundred years have now been drawn to the surface, in full view and stripped to essentials, by the Manchurian affair. Those forces must

be resolved or they must march to their logical conclusion. But they cannot be understood, dealt with, or
resolved unless they are seen as innate in the cultural
evolution of the last century and a half and in the
modern system—our nationalistic, economic, social
system. To think of them in terms of politics alone,
in terms of "foreign affairs," international relations,
even of *Weltpolitik*, is restricted and futile, as our efforts to "solve" the Manchurian incident were futile.
For that is to ignore all the sources, the deeper springs,
of group action in the times in which we live. In other
words, we cannot deal with the Far East without dealing with ourselves. We cannot settle the conflict in the
East without easing the strains in our own society.
An inquiry into the affairs of the Far East is in equal
part an inquiry into the nature of our own social order.

As we look at the Far East now, we see China arrayed against the Western powers and Japan to the end
of recovering its independence. It has had varying
fortunes, in the first decade after the World War having
considerable success and in the years since 1929 suffering severe reverses, notably the loss of Manchuria. But
that the struggle will go on, now relaxing, now intensifying, is inevitable. Either China must ultimately evict
all those who have encroached on its territory and
independence and achieve a status of full equality
among the nations, or it must be effectually conquered
by a single power or a group of powers. The last few
years have demonstrated that in order to retain even a
degree of dominance over China any or all of the foreign
powers must have full dominion. Imperial rule by threat
of potential force is no longer effective against a rebel-

lious dependency. The hypnosis exercised by the white nations in non-white territories throughout the last century has lost its potency. For any nation to retain any of its present rights in China it is necessary to do as Japan did in Manchuria after 1931.

As we look at the Far East we see also the great powers arrayed against one another over their respective ambitions in China, principally Russia against Japan, the United States against Japan. The others are less involved only by degree. Now, no nation is ever motivated by a desire for war, in the Far East or anywhere else. It is only driven by inner needs—or what its ruling groups conceive to be needs—to actions which bring it into collision with other nations. Japan believes it must have Manchuria as an outlet for economic expansion—as a reservoir of raw materials and a market for the surplus factory products it must sell to support its people. To the same end it believes it must have overlordship in all of northeastern Asia. Soviet Russia is already entrenched in northeastern Asia, however, and will not recede; it has reason to believe, that, if it did, Japan would be only emboldened to push further. The United States, while never clearly declaring itself, or, perhaps, even clearly conscious of its position, refuses to permit China to be preëmpted as a field for economic exploitation by any power.

The motives of the United States are mixed, as well as unexpressed and not consciously reasoned, but that the main ingredient of the mixture is self-interest can hardly be denied by any who read history and are not romantic in their view of history. There is little that is capricious, impulsive, sentimental, or accidental in the position we have repeatedly assumed in the Far East. When a nation acts consistently in any situation over a long period, it is not actuated by whimsicality or momentary feeling. Since 1900 the United States has acted consistently in the Far East. In fact, never since then has it deviated from a straight line of action. No matter who was President and who were in his cabinet, no matter what their origin, their party, their political and economic convictions, their cast of mind and temperament, they have all responded in exactly the same way to the situations put by the Far East. Whether the Secretary of State was Elihu Root or Philander Knox or Henry L. Stimson, or their anti-type, William Jennings Bryan, all have followed the same course of conduct with respect to the Far East, even if their verbal reasons varied. They may have differed over states rights, the tariff, trusts, labor laws, literature, liquor, and religion, but they have agreed on the Far East. Indeed, they have agreed on almost nothing else. Whatever the composition of the American government, it has unswervingly opposed the effort of any power to conquer, dominate, or control China or take a lien on its opportunities for development. Whether its stand was taken in the name of the Open Door or the integrity of China or the sanctity of anti-war treaties, this has been the purport and the net result of its action. For this has been its policy: that China shall remain a free field for American economic enterprise. Considered as a generalization, such a policy may be justified. But similar policies in other areas, equally valid as generalizations, have not been pursued with equal vigor and consistency. The

United States is not animated by abstract concepts. It is moved by the desire for an opportunity for its own economic expansion in China, the most fertile field for economic expansion still remaining open.

American interest in the Far East was sporadic and casual until the closing years of the nineteenth century —that is, until our own frontiers had passed and internal development could no longer absorb all our energies. Then for the first time we were free to turn our thoughts outward. And just then we launched our career in the Pacific by annexing Hawaii and taking the Philippines from Spain. Thus we became a Pacific Power, and immediately thereupon we assumed the sponsorship of the Open Door Doctrine for China, our first positive entrance into Far Eastern world politics. We have never withdrawn. To the contrary, we have pressed farther in. From the first pronouncement of the Open Door Doctrine in 1899 to our assumption of international leadership in opposing Japan's absorption of Manchuria in 1932 our course has been direct and clear, ever more positive, ever more assertive, ever more forceful. When Russia was the most menacing aggressor against China we opposed Russia. In the Russo-Japanese War we were pro-Japanese to the point of sentimentality. Japan evicted Russia and took over its ambitions for hegemony in the Far East. Almost immediately we began protesting against Japan's actions in Manchuria, we adumbrated schemes for neutralizing or internationalizing Manchurian railways, and in less than five years tensions had arisen between Japan and the United States. The tensions have never eased. Instead, they have become exacerbated. To every effort by Japan to encroach farther on the Asiatic continent the United States has stood squarely in obstruction: in 1915, on the occasion of the Twenty-one Demands; in 1919, over Shantung; in 1920–21, over Siberia; in 1921–22, at the Washington Conference; since 1931, over Manchuria. With each occasion the antagonism has become aggravated and the issue more starkly defined.

It is the fond belief of the American people that save for the aberration of 1917, subsequently atoned, they have been faithful to George Washington's injunction against foreign entanglements. Vis-à-vis Europe we may have kept the faith. In Asia we are most definitely entangled, and we have been for many years, even before the repented adventure in Europe. The truth has been obscured to us by the fact that our rôle has not been that of contender for territory, as with other imperialistic powers. We do not aspire to territory. We do not have to. We have ample room for our population, and we are practically self-sufficient in natural resources. Our need is rather for a market for the surplus goods made possible by our high productivity and for opportunity to invest the surplus capital arising from the same source. Our stake in empire is not territory but a free field for economic expansion. This is one reason for our variation from imperialistic type. The other is that, since we entered the world arena, imperial conquest has become more oblique and subtle. Possession of alien territory is no longer essential; it may even be a disadvantage. Economic control is enough.

The struggle for mastery in the Far East has not

abated. To the contrary, it has intensified. With the Manchurian incident it approaches determination. With that incident, also, the United States became unmistakably, definitively engaged in the struggle. The East has been drawn into the Western system. The United States has been drawn into the system of world politics. In both cases the magnetism of the underlying forces of the time has been irresistible. These are the forces released by scientific discovery, mechanization, power-machine industry, and credit capitalism. They made both possible and inevitable the thrust of the West on the East, and against the weight they put behind the thrust, the East was helpless. And after America had reached a certain stage in its economic development it, too, was pulled out of its course into the world stream. It, too, has been helpless.

Presumably we do not want to resign ourselves to waiting fatalistically for the struggle to be pressed to decision and the whole world to drift helpless into a whirlpool of Asiatic wars. If so, there are definite choices to be made. There is no reason in historical precedent or on the evidence in the Far East to expect that the existing forces can progress in their present direction and momentum without international collision. If that is to be averted, they must be given new direction, neutralized, altered, or arrested. In pure reason the simplest solution is withdrawal from the struggle. The powers would have to retire, then, from economic competition in China—competition for trade, for the opportunity to make loans, for investments in exploiting the country's mines, building railroads, establishing public utilities. Only in pure reason is this simple: there is, indeed, no obstacle in natural law. In actuality it has only to be stated to be dismissed. We would not do so if we could; and we cannot. The same forces that made us get into the Far East prevent us from getting out. Never were they more compelling than now, and never was the compulsion more evident.

The social and economic order of the West in the last hundred years was built up by exploiting the five continents of their resources and selling to the untouched markets of the world the goods that the new demands created by the industrial system called for. The industrialization of Europe and America alone would not have enabled us to erect the imposing structure of our great cities, our public services, our social services, our accumulations of capital, and the vast system of credit. Had there been only the wants of Europe and America to fill, we should have reached a static point in the West long before the post-war period. Instead, England reached out into Asia and then Africa, followed by the other nations as they industrialized. Both the grandeur and power of the British Empire were founded on the textile trade of the East; its financial supremacy was founded on the profits of that trade, reinvested at home or exported abroad in the form of loans or investments in foreign basic industries or transportation systems. So it was also with the rest of western Europe, and so it is beginning to be with the United States, now that we are at saturation point at home. Our command of the backward or industrially undeveloped parts of the earth gave us our wealth and power and pomp, and equally what we call our advancement in the more intangible, less material aspects of our civilization.

This is no less true today, even if it takes directions unanticipated in the hundred years of booster psychology and booster economics—boosterism in England and France and Germany no less than in the raw American chamber of commerce West, even if less blatant. For one thing, we are coming to saturation point anyway. The backward countries are themselves industrializing, as might have been expected had not our superman psychosis hypnotized ourselves as completely as it did the non-white peoples we cowed. The backward peoples are industrializing, and we shall lose, therefore, not our foreign trade altogether but the bonanza profit therefrom, as in the nineteenth century. But it is just now, when we can least afford to lose it, that we are threatened with its loss. For just now, for reasons innate in our own situation, we are desperately in need of trade.

So far from relinquishing our prospects of increased opportunities for economic enterprise in the Far East, we are more likely to enter on a desperate race for markets. Given the projection of the existing social forces, we must. It is not a matter now of building up family financial dynasties or world-wide corporations. It is a matter of disposing of our surplus products, so that we may keep our factories running and our workers employed. It is a matter of survival, not of profits. Once decision on the question of economic penetration and empire may have been an abstract speculation or an ethical consideration; today it determines preservation or decline of our social order and the civilization on which it rests. Given the existing order, we have no

choice but to enter on a trade war in all parts of the
world. We must also keep a free field for investments.
In the first place, surplus capital must always find an
outlet. When the law of diminishing returns sets in at
home, it will seek higher return abroad. It is assumed
now that we shall continue to have surplus profits. If
not, the old order will have gone, in any case. Furthermore, investments in prospective markets are the surest
guaranty of possession of the markets. In fact, there is
no other guaranty. Unless the British had poured millions into South African mines and the railways, harbors, roads, and all that accompanies the first stage in
development, they would have sold only a negligible
quantity of goods in South Africa. This is why the
Japanese have insisted on priority in loans to Manchuria. If they build and control the railways and
harbors, the mines and mills and banks, it is their
machinery and cotton goods that will be bought. At
least, so it has been all through the period of empire.
We must, then, have a trade war and a war of financial
penetration.

This has long been foreshadowed. Its outlines could
be traced even before the World War. In fact, the
sharpening of competition between the British and
Germans in the Near East and Far East was in large
part responsible for the war, or for the exacerbation of
rancors which had to eventuate in war. Since the World
War it has been clearly visible in all parts of the world.
Japan seeks to close off northern China for itself; the
United States stands opposed. More direct evidence is
the controversy between Great Britain and Japan in
the last two years, since Japan has been making inroads

into British trade in India. In effect, the war for trade is already on. That trade wars cannot long be waged without enlarging into wars on the battlefield is axiomatic. We are now in the preliminary stages of fencing with tariffs, currencies, quotas. The next stage is that of naval races and rivalry for naval bases, cable landings, and strategic outposts. In the next come alliances and counter alliances, with diplomatic maneuvering, jockeying for position, and the identification of national honor and prestige with technical moves on a diplomatic checkerboard.

Then we have the setting for "incidents" and a background of mass emotions which can be touched off by such incidents, after which statesmen are swept along, recking then for the first time of the dangers with which they have been playing. Some such incident was conceivable in 1932, when Secretary of State Stimson was sending edged notes to Tokyo and Japanese shells were falling around the American Marine barracks and the American School in Shanghai. Had a shell hit . . . !

A similar incident is more than conceivable now on the Siberian border, where Japanese and Russian troops face each other. If mass emotions do not touch off spontaneously, they can also be fired. The machinery of propaganda to hand for the controlling group in any country is now so smoothly efficient, the means of playing on the mass mind and emotions are so skillful, so subtle and so easy to bring into play, that any nation can be regimented quickly, easily, and effectively for any purpose desired by those who wield power. The press, the radio, the moving picture, advertising, the "drive"—all are irresistible, even by the wary. Of course, the American people do not want war with Japan. Neither do the people of Japan want war with America. The people—the inhabitants of any country as so many individuals—never spontaneously want war. But the desire can fuse within them when the constituent elements are given. If necessary, it can be manufactured. The argument that the American people do not want war is unanswerable. It is also pointless. They will want war when necessary, or they will be made to want it. Whether there is war against Japan or any other nation does not depend on their thoughts and desires and feelings now, but on whether the causes are allowed to form and grow.

In the nature of our society we of the West cannot literally get out of the Far East. The United States cannot extricate itself from the Far Eastern welter. It was drawn in by its own social evolution, and all the evidence of the last few years is that it is getting in deeper. Our society being what it is, we can only stay in, with the consequence that the conflict already set in will develop until it comes to climax in formal wars. If, under our present society, we cannot get out and cannot stay in without advancing irresistibly toward wars, the only alternative is to change the content and the direction of the motive forces in our society so that we shall not be compelled to engage in competition for economic advantages in distant parts in order to keep our economic system in equilibrium: we shall not, in other words, be driven fatalistically into the race for empire.

In effect, this entails the recasting of our social forms. It means the denial of the right of private interests to embark on financial enterprises in other parts of the world bearing with them the support of their governments and, by inference, the pledge of their countrymen in war to back up their efforts. It means control over the movements of private capital to other parts of the world. Further, and more important, it means the reorganization of our domestic economy so that it will no longer be necessary to find outlets, by means of national "policies," for surplus production and surplus capital. From this it follows that we must control both the accumulation of capital and, if necessary, the production of goods. We need not necessarily compel a quantitative restriction of either. We need only change the disposition and use of surplus. Instead of using it for reinvestment and export, so that there may be more wealth accumulated to be reinvested in more productive machinery to make more goods to be exported for more profit and so on, we shall turn it back for more intensive cultivation at home. By increasing the economic return to labor, which is to say setting up a new principle of distribution of wealth by enforcing a limit on profits, we shall consume at home what now constitutes excess production. Such excess wealth as still inures to us by virtue of our high productivity and continued scientific advancement will be devoted to social uses: more security, more leisure, greater ease, ampler enjoyments, and the multiplicity of activities unrelated to the making of salable commodities. We shall not measure progress only by economic expansion, by quantitative increase. That this entails fundamental changes in the social and economic system is self-evident. But that drastic and fundamental changes are coming in any case is also self-evident: either changes or catastrophe. The question is only in what manner they shall come: with or without revolution, before or after a series of wars. For they are as clearly a corollary of the invention of machinery as is mass production—or international rivalry for markets.

The Far Eastern problem has a broader basis than the Far East; its solution cannot be found in the Far East alone. It is a product of the disparity in the cultural development of the two hemispheres in the last hundred and fifty years. Out of the disparity and the disproportionate distribution of material power that resulted came the successful efforts of the nations of the West to reduce those of the East, China in particular, to subjection and use them for exploitation. Because of our organization in competitive nationalistic units there came also rivalries for the perquisites of exploitation. And our later social evolution makes those perquisites indispensable to the maintenance of our system.

To restore peace in the East and equilibrium in the relation of East and West it is necessary to redress that disparity or neutralize its effects. The first is already in train. The East is modernizing—that is, industrializing. Whatever form the culture of China ultimately takes, it will be, at least in externals, in tune with the modern world: either that, or there will be no China. Meanwhile the effects of the disparity must be neutralized. China must be left free to find its own way into the modern world and move to its destination at its own pace, however often it stumbles or slips back, and even if it appears to be making no progress: this out of no altruism or "friendship" for China but as a measure of self-preservation, of prevention of wars for the right of ascendancy. Also, we must so reshape our social system that we shall not be compelled to take advantage of the disparity by political aggressions for economic aggrandizement. Thus, and thus alone, can the Far East be eliminated as a theater of war. For only thus can the causes of war in the Far East be removed. Stimson Doctrines, Kellogg Pacts, League Covenants, the technique of peace by conference, rhetorical formulae and idealism in words—these are futile. While the causes of war remain, they will have effect in war.

The Far East states in its own terms the whole social problem of our time. In origin and evolution the Far Eastern problem is a Western problem, a European-American problem. Its solution lies primarily in the West, not in the East. The primary factors are not political but social and cultural.

THE AUTHORS

THE AUTHORS

O WEN LATTIMORE, explorer, who has spent most of his life in China, Mongolia, and Turkistan, is the author of *The Desert Road to Turkistan* and *Manchuria, Cradle of Conflict*. John E. Orchard, Associate Professor at Columbia University, has specialized on problems of industry in the Orient; author of *Japan's Economic Position*. Joseph Barnes, secretary of the American Council of the Institute of Pacific Relations, has lived and traveled extensively in the Soviet Union. Grover Clark, former editor of the *Peking Leader*, has lived for many years in China, and is a specialist on China's economic problems. Frederick V. Field, author of *American Participation in the China Consortiums*, was formerly Secretary to the International Research Committee of the Institute of Pacific Relations. H. Foster Bain, former director of the United States Bureau of Mines, is the author of *Ores and Minerals in the Far*

THE AUTHORS

East. Carl L. Alsberg, former chief of the United States Bureau of Chemistry, is the Director of the Food Research Institute at Stanford University. Pearl S. Buck, author of *The Good Earth,* has lived most of her life in China, part of it in close relation to the mission movement. Tyler Dennett, professor of International Relations at Princeton, former historical adviser to the Department of State, has recently published the definitive life of John Hay. Nathaniel Peffer, author of *The White Man's Dilemma* and *China: The Collapse of a Civilization,* was for many years a newspaper correspondent in the Far East.